THE ULTIMATE LIFESTYLE

**VISION HOUSE
PUBLISHERS**

Santa Ana, California 92705

The Ultimate Lifestyle

Copyright © 1977 by Vision House Publishers, Santa Ana, California 92705.

Library of Congress Catalog Card Number 77-20594
ISBN Number 0-88449-027-0

Printed in the United States of America.

TO

David G. Canine—whose responsible and compassionate life originally motivated me toward seeking the ultimate lifestyle.

ACKNOWLEDGEMENTS

A special thanks goes to . . .

Martha Kimmell, for her invaluable support as my research and editorial assistant.

George Busiek, Don Edney, Willard Thompson, Earl Fain, Mike Crain, and *John Saville* for their encouragement and interaction in the early stages of development of this material.

Toby Walker for his genuine friendship, loving motivation and fresh realism.

Roy and *Janis Coffee* and *Don* and *Janie McKay* for a constant demonstration of "Salt and Light" in their community.

Peggy Nighswonger for her helpful feedback and typing of the manuscript.

CONTENTS

A NOTE TO SKEPTICS

NATURAL—1. of, forming a part of, or arising from nature; in accordance with what is found or expected in nature.[1] *SUPERNATURAL*—1. existing or occurring outside the normal experience or knowledge of man . . . 2. the intervention of supernatural forces in nature.[2]

The two most basic philosophies of life rest on these foundations—the natural and the supernatural. The naturalistic philosophy (e.g. humanism, rationalism, existentialism) is a pattern of thought holding to the principle that events occur uniformly within a closed system. All things continue according to the laws of nature just as they always have. This could be illustrated by a circle drawn alone on an infinite canvas with all events taking place inside the circle. As man continues in the slow process of evolution he can find reality only in this circle. He is limited to finding meaning for his life from within the circle, and reasoning from this naturalistic base he is impervious to any supernatural intervention. He reasons in a closed system: "Miracles don't happen, because they can't happen! God doesn't exist because He can't exist!"

The supernaturalistic philosophy is a pattern of thought holding to the principle that events occur uniformly, but in an open system. All things continue according to the laws of nature just as they always have, but there is the possibility of intrusion from an outside source. This *supernatural* source does not break the laws of nature but may alter them by intervention. This system is open since it does not limit man to himself, but allows for that which is beyond nature or man's knowledge and experience—the supernatural.

These two philosophies of life lead to two very different ends. The naturalistic philosophy taken to its logical end concludes that man is nothing more than a part of the great cosmic machinery. The supernaturalistic philosophy taken to its logical end concludes that man is significant because he is separate from, not part of the machine.

For a time the naturalistic philosophy had high hopes for man. "Basic to the humanistic mentality of Western man since the Renaissance has been the belief in the inherent goodness of man and inevitability of his progress. These grand assumptions have been shattered and widely abandoned because of the shocking revelations of man's inhumanity to man in the twentieth century, and the slow realization of the fundamental hopelessness of a naturalistic philosophy."[3] The hopelessness of the naturalistic philosophy can be easily explained. "Matter plus time plus chance equals zero! If man is the illegitimate offspring of a thoughtless parent order, the mockery of fortuitous chance, his significance is nil. There is no conceivable way to construct a meaningful dwelling for man upon the uncongenial foundations of chaos and accident."[4]

Destined for high hopes, naturalistic man has dwindled to an insignificant accident. In his book, *The Ghost in the Machine*, Arthur Koestler concludes: "It appears highly probable that Homo Sapiens is a biological freak, the result of some remarkable mistake in the evolutionary process."[5] Nobel Prize winner Jacques Monod writes: "Our number came up in a Monte Carlo game. Is it any wonder if, like the person who has just made a million at the casino, we feel strange and a little unreal?"[6] Monod concludes his book *Chance and Necessity*: "The ancient covenant [between man and the universe] is in pieces; man knows at last that he is alone in the universe's unfeeling immensity, out of which he emerged only by chance. His destiny is nowhere spelled out, nor is his duty."[7]

The naturalistic philosophy is faced with a runaway, machine-like world which lacks meaning and a sense of morality, "No one—not even the most brilliant scientist alive today—really knows where science is taking us. We are aboard a train which is gathering speed, racing down a track on which there are an unknown number of switches leading to unknown destinations. No single scientist is in the engine cab and there may be demons at the switch. Most of society is in the caboose looking backward."[8] The philosophy of naturalism recognizes no limits or boundaries. If something can be done, then it must be done regardless of the result. Morality is reduced to sociological probabilities. Whatever a person thinks is right is right. Since he is only a product of change (a machine), what makes the difference?

No meaning! No morality! No reality! No purpose! John Lennon came to this point of despair and said: "The dream is over. I'm not just talking about the generation thing. It's over and we gotta—I have personally gotta—get down to so-called reality."[9] One of the most articulate expressions of the despair of naturalistic philosophy has been in the "theatre of the absurd." This is a group of playwrights committed to portraying in dramatic form the total emptiness of life. Samuel Beckett represented their thinking when he said, "How am I, an a-temporal being imprisoned in time and space, to escape from my imprisonment, when I know that outside space and time lies nothing, and that I, in the ultimate depths of my reality am Nothing also?"[10]

In the philosophy of naturalism (trapped in a closed system of events) God does not exist, man lives only to become non-existent, and all life is destined for death. All that continues is the cold, cosmic machinery grinding away as it always has. Man must either accept his insignificance as part of the machine or be mangled in the gears.

Despite its appeal and seeming validity, man does not easily accept the conclusion of naturalism. There is an innate unwillingness to succumb to it and an unending struggle to negate it, to leap out of the closed system into the dark, out of reality into non-reality, away from reason into non-reason.

This leap into the dark may take any of a number of forms: drugs, the occult, meditation, and varied religious experiences. All of these are used as vehicles in the search for reality and meaning to life. Who am I? Why am I? The leap into the dark is a search for the *supernatural*—that which is beyond the natural. It's a craving for anything outside the cosmic machinery which may have meaning that a person might cling to. Sometimes these leaps into darkness do result in "meaningful" experience, but they don't fit with reality for practical day to day living.

The blind leaps, the feeling of despair and struggle for meaningful identity are not experienced only by the philosophers of the world. All levels of society are affected: (1) The business executive who feels the utter futility of climbing the corporate ladder. Beaten down by the stresses of his profession he asks, "Was it worth it?" (2) The housewife who is sick of the pressurized rat race of life and asks, "Is this all there is to life?" (3) The university student who feels he is just another number. (4) The man working on the assembly line who has been replaced by a computer. (5) The 65-year old man who has been forced by "the system" to retire, only to die a year later. (6) The citizen who has been given the bureaucratic run-around by an impersonal governmental system. (7) The person all alone in a crowd wondering if anyone really cares.

Every person feels despair and meaninglessness at some point in his life and each reacts in a different way. Some try to ignore it by becoming busy in the affairs of life only to be shocked into reality by various tragedies. Some revolt and break their traditional molds. Some kill themselves. Others reject reality altogether and live in institutions. An increasing number of people are retreating to a more simplified mode of life. Others are trying various leaps into the dark. Each is on a search, whether it be passive or aggressive—a search for meaning and reality in everyday practical living.

Christianity offers a solution to man's search! You may say, "Wait a minute. I've heard it all before!" But have you? Arnold Toynbee said, "People have not rejected true Christianity, but only a poor caricature of it." You see, true Christianity repudiates the leap in the dark as foolishness and presents a lifestyle of significance and meaning. It's a lifestyle that can be lived effectively in this meaningless, chaotic world, and it contains a confident hope that can be communicated to a hopeless, terminal generation. It's *The Ultimate Lifestyle!*

Christianity rejects the narrow philosophy of naturalism and embraces the more liberal (open-minded) philosophy of supernaturalism.[11] Christian supernaturalism believes that there is a personal, transcendent (not a part of nature) God who is responsible for the creation of man. Because the supernatural God created him uniquely, man is distinct from the plants and animals or nature itself. There is something special about man in that he is created in the image of God—he has personality as does God. This sets man apart from the natural, non-personal, world-system, yet he functions within it. Only man can have a supernatural, personal relationship with the supernatual, personal God of the universe. The philosophy of Christian supernaturalism is dedicated to the fact that this supernatural, personal God is actively involved in the affairs of human beings today and has a purpose for man in the future. Both of these truths are revealed in the Bible.

The Ultimate Lifestyle is an attempt to define and illustrate how the infinite, supernatural, personal God of the universe and a finite, personal man can establish and maintain a supernatural relationship in the midst of a sick and dying naturalistic world. *The Ultimate Lifestyle* is the genuine Christian lifestyle!

There is a three-fold challenge underlying this book: (1) *to the naturalist*, to think about and give honest consideration to the Christian lifestyle stripped of its caricatures; (2) *to the non-Christian supernaturalist*, to face the fact that his philosophy is based on a counterfeit of the supernatural God of the universe; and (3) *to the Christian supernaturalist*, to model his lifestyle so that it demonstrates that he is distinctively in touch with the supernatural God and evidences this relationship to his fellow man.

INTRODUCTION

"If Christianity were a crime, would there be enough evidence to convict you?" I never did like that question. Christianity is not a crime, so why discuss it? Hypothetical questions annoy me. But one day while I was mentally attempting to file this question under "hypothetical-impractical," I realized there might possibly be a deeper reason for my rejecting it. In my heart I didn't want to face the issue of searching for the reality of God in my life. Too many uncomfortable questions came to mind: Is there anything in my life that couldn't be explained psychologically? Is there any real evidence that I am experiencing anything different than a Buddhist or Moslem or a man worshipping some inanimate object? Is there anything supernatural about my life? Is God really there? I was afraid to confront myself with these questions. The answer to all of them might be a cold, eternal No. I couldn't face that possibility. It could be devastating! After all, I was in the ministry!

Spiritual Nausea

If my experience of Christianity lacked the supernatural dimension of life revealed in the Bible, then either I had missed it or it wasn't there to be found. I had heard all the spiritual clichés and quickie formulas prescribed as cure-alls to honest and many times painful problems: "Let go and let God!" "Trust the Lord with it!" "What you need is to be filled with the Spirit!" "Have you had the baptism of the Spirit?" "Do you have any known sin in your life?" "It's the Lord's problem!" "Pray about it!" "You need to get involved in personal evangelism!" Compelled by the hunger for reality in my life and filled with spiritual nausea I began craving the supernatural God.

Because I had counseled individuals extensively over the past eight years, I knew I wasn't alone in my search. On the contrary, nearly every person with whom I've counseled is suffering to some degree from the same predicament—a gnawing uncertainty of the reality of God in his daily experience. No matter what the person's immediate problem is, there is still that underlying, unsettled question: "How can I know the supernatural God of the Bible?"

The Swinging Pendulum

There are two extreme answers to this very valid question, and both indicate a high degree of arrogance. One is the position that God can be known by content alone. "Learn all the Bible doctrine and theology possible. Then you'll know God." Certainly the content of the revealed Word of God is necessary, but content alone without the context of experience produces cold, dead orthodoxy. It's stuffy! Paul warns the Corinthians that "knowledge makes arrogant" people (I Corinthians 8:1). He tells Timothy that "in the last days difficult times will come" and people will be "always learning and never able to come to the knowledge of the truth" (II Timothy 3:1, 7).

The other arrogant extreme proposes that God can be known by experience alone. This approach is usually characterized by seeking deeper experiences with God with very little regard to the content of His revealed Word. Again Paul warns the Corinthians "not to exceed [go beyond] what is written, in order that no one of you might become arrogant in behalf of one against the other" (I Corinthians 4:6).

These two approaches arise as reactions against one another. The pendulum swings from extreme to extreme—in opposing one extreme, people tend to move to the other. When reacting against knowledge they swing to the side of experience and when reacting against experience they swing to the side of knowledge. The more firmly a person seems set in either extreme, the more likely he is to swing to the opposite one. Both are dangerously wrong and both are anti-Christian.

Experience-Only

There has been a strong tendency in our generation to move toward the experience-only extreme. One reason for this is intellectual intimidation Christians experience in the face of the pervading existential mood of our world. For many years Christians in general have been unable to give adequate answers in the areas of science, philosophy, psychology, etc. The scholars and intellects were continually asking questions that were threatening to the very foundation of Christianity. Instead of grappling with these questions, studying to discover the Bible's adequate answers, most Christians developed a defensive attitude, ridiculing that which is intellectual and retreating from the battleground of thought and content. They have concluded, "My experience with God is all I need!"

In one sense, of course, this is true. But when a person rejects the intellectual content that governs his experience, the door is opened widely to the dangers of the experience-only extreme. When it comes to defending why your experience is more valid than that of a member of the Hare Krishna sect or of a young man seeking God through drugs or of a witch who experiences her "control" spirit, you have a problem. How can you demonstrate that your experience with the supernatural God of the universe is any better than theirs? You can't! Without understanding the intellectual content of His revealed Word it is impossible.

Instant Breakfast

Another reason for the current shift toward the experience-only extreme is the thorough saturation of our society by existentialism. Existentialism encourages the "instant breakfast" approach to life. The mood is captured in such expressions as "I want to feel it!" or "I want to experience it—now!"

The shift toward the experience-only extreme is quite subtle. The innocent search for reality in the Christian's life may turn into a dangerous, blind search for the supernatural. The Bible clearly states that we should come to *know* the Lord better. Paul reveals his heart's desire to the Philippians: "That I may *know* Him" (Philippians 3:10). He exhorts the Ephesians to build up one another toward the attainment of the "*knowledge* of the Son of God, to a mature man, to the measure of the stature which belongs to the fulness of Christ" (Ephesians 4:13). Peter urges us to "grow in the grace and *knowledge* of our Lord and Savior Jesus Christ" (II Peter 3:18). Since the biblical word *knowledge*, when it is used of a relationship, emphasizes experiencing the other person, it is easy to make the dangerous shift. The "knowing" aspect of knowledge is ignored and only the "experiencing" aspect is appreciated. The search for the reality of God becomes a search for a certain experience. This can turn into a search for anything supernatural, anything that is outside of the person and beyond his powers. The risk at this point is extremely high, for there is another supernatural force in the world—an evil one. And that force can deceive us with counterfeit experiences.[1]

Knowledge-Only

On the other hand, the knowledge-only extreme can be equally dangerous. In some ways it is more subtle. Experience can obviously be filled with faulty content (or none at all), therefore, it's easy to be suspicious of someone's experience. However, the knowledge-only extreme appears to be based upon the most genuine content available to man—the written revelation of God, the Bible. How can a person go wrong? After all, he is using "the Word." Nevertheless, it is very possible and quite common for a person to have cognitive knowledge without experiential knowledge. He may know all about God, but not actually know God. He may know all about the Bible without knowing the life and power of the Word in his daily life.

This extreme of knowledge-only breeds a pharisaical approach to the Christian life. Christianity is wrapped up tightly in a neat package by lists of do's and don't's. Many of the lists have very little to do with the Bible, but are motivated by culture and tradition. Culture and tradition are treated as absolutes equal to the revelation of God. These cultural and traditional "absolutes" cause the true biblical absolutes to be of little effect.

The spirit of pharisaism is often accompanied by an attitude of anti-supernaturalism. It is true that much of what is labeled "supernatural" today has another more natural explanation to it or may even be demonic. But the knowledge-only extreme tries to place God in a box where He can be predicted and controlled. I'm convinced that most knowledge-only extremists would not recognize a miracle if they saw it. (It's a good thing that the Rapture will be a sovereign act of God. Otherwise, some of these people would probably balk at that future supernatural event!) The knowledge-only extreme must be avoided at all cost. It's just as anti-Christian as the experience-only extreme. Both are distortions and neither reflects the balance and the beauty that God offers.

One factor which adds to the tendency toward the two extremes is the misuse of what the Bible says. This misuse can take three different forms: (1) overemphasis of certain content of the Word; (2) misunderstanding of the content; or (3) misapplication of the content. These three forms overlap and interrelate in such a way that it is often difficult to identify a specific misuse of the Bible in a given situation.

Examples of misuse of the Bible are numerous. A common one is the popular teaching on miracles. From some Christian writings you get the overwhelming impression that the Bible is full of the miraculous and that if your life is right with God, you should be experiencing miracles each day. Lack of faith in a miracle-working God is given as the reason why people are physically and spiritually sick. Yet when we closely examine the Bible on the subject of miracles, we find that quite the contrary is true. God performed miracles in the "showy" kind of way during periods amounting to only 125 to 150 years in all of history! This occurred primarily during the time of Moses, Elijah, Elisha, Daniel, and Jesus and His disciples. The purpose of these "showy" demonstrations of the supernatural was evidently to authenticate God's revelation to man at significant times in history. Rather than being the *norm* of life, the "showy" miracles are clearly the *exception* in the history of mankind.

Another common example of the misuse of Biblical content by overemphasis, misunderstanding, or misapplication is in the matter of discovering the will of God. Voluminous material exists on how to find God's will for your life. It may be exciting to review all the many insights that have been written on such a vital subject as this, but it is interesting that the one Book we would expect to speak to the issue does not say we are to seek God's will. The Bible says we should "know" it (as if there is a body of teaching where it can be found), places a great emphasis on "doing" it (as if we could easily know it), but does not say we should seek it. This indicates that God's will is not mysterious and elusive.

Cycle of Disintegration

These and many other examples will be brought into biblical focus as we attempt to search for the supernatural God, the content in our experience. By establishing a true biblical base for our experience, we will be able to live *The Ultimate Lifestyle*. This lifestyle will not only face up to reality, but it will stand out in the world in which we live. The world has no standard by which to measure what is right or wrong, good or bad. People in this world-system without a Biblical base are caught in a cycle of disintegration: (1) "It all depends on how you look at it!" (2) "It doesn't make any difference how you look at it." (3) "No one knows how to look at it!" This cycle permeates all of life—values, morals, etc.

In the face of the utter despair and groping for reality prevalent in the world-system today, the Christian must stand in stark contrast. He must display true reality and offer genuine hope to those around him. Reality and hope are founded on a meaningful, personal relationship with the supernatural God. You can't display true reality or offer genuine hope to the world unless you know the reality of God in your daily experience and are confident of His work in *your* life!

The Ultimate Lifestyle tells a story—a story of one person's struggle to experience the reality of God in his daily life and to evidence that reality to the world. It's the product of struggling with problems, both mine and others', and of wrestling with the God of the Bible over the gnawing questions of everyday life.

The Ultimate Lifestyle is for those who are hungering and thirsting for a genuine experience of the supernatural God. Balanced and practical answers to four questions will provide the needed insight for you to enjoy the supernatural relationship and to evidence it to your world: (1) What is the Christian lifestyle? (2) Who lives it? (3) Where is it lived? (4) How is it lived?

FOOTNOTES

A Note To Skeptics

1. *Webster's New World Dictionary of the American Language* (Cleveland and New York: The World Publishing Company, 1968), p. 977.
2. Ibid., p. 1464.
3. Clark H. Pinnock, *Set Forth Your Case* (Chicago: Moody Press, 1967), p. 9.
4. Ibid., p. 19.
5. Os Guinness, *The Dust of Death* (Downers Grove: Inter-Varsity Press, 1973), p. 156.
6. Jacques Monod, *Chance and Necessity* (New York: Knopf, 1971), p. 146.
7. Ibid., p. 180.
8. Ralph Lapp, quoted in Guinness, op. cit., p. 67.
9. Ibid., p. 76 (Quoted from John Lennon).
10. Richard Coe, quoted in Pinnock, op. cit., p. 18.
11. Supernaturalism has other forms—occultism, Satanism, cultic splits off of Christianity, etc. Some of these forms will be discussed as counterfeits of Christianity in Chapter IX.

Introduction

1. Further discussion of this may be found in Part Two. I also refer you to my book. *Chains of the Spirit: A Manual for Liberation* (Grand Rapids, MI: Baker Book House, n.d.).

Part One

PERSPECTIVE—WHAT IS THE ULTIMATE LIFESTYLE?

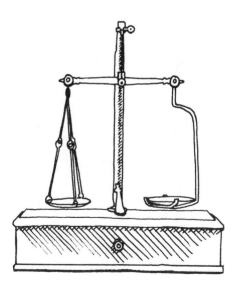

One

CHRISTIANITY: RELIGION OR RELATIONSHIP?

"Christianity is not a religion, it's a relationship with God through Jesus Christ." That may be the most unethical propaganda ever used to evangelize people into Christianity. It is not unethical because of its falsehood—on the contrary, it is absolutely true! And it is not unethical because of its insignificance—it is most significant! But this statement borders on being unethical propaganda because of the fact that it is not being demonstrated in the lives of the believers.

Sailboat Without a Sail

It's like trying to sell a sailboat without a sail. The newspaper ad called it a sailboat. The description strongly implied it was a sailboat with a sail. The buyer certainly thought he was buying a sailboat with a sail. The boat was designed to have a sail, but it just isn't there. You can row the boat. You can use a motor. You can even call it a sailboat, but until you get the sail and put it in its place, you cannot sail in your sailboat.

Frequently an unsuspecting person enters into a relationship with God through Jesus Christ and becomes very, very religious. As a new believer he is instructed to be at the proper worship services, sit in the proper pew, read the proper books, attend the "in" seminars, Bible studies, and prayer groups. By the time he has participated in all of the "spiritual" activities, he's near exhaustion. Is this a relationship? Hardly!

Suppose I were to tell you that my wife and I have a dynamic relationship and that it functions in this way: We wake up in the morning about 6:30 and I say, "Honey, tonight from 6:00 to 6:35 is your time with me. Be there!" A relationship? No! Maybe an acquaintance, but certainly not a relationship! Believers treat the Lord the same way with a "nod to God" approach to Christianity. That simply is not a relationship. It's just another religion called Christianity. It's as dead as the body of Lazarus, and could be described in the same terms, "Behold, how it stinketh!" True Christianity was never meant to be another religion, but a dynamic relationship with God through Jesus Christ. Anything short of a demonstration of that relationship between the holy God of the universe and sinful man cannot and must not be called Christianity.

An Example at Ephesus

There was a church in the first century that lost the struggle of religion vs. relationship. The church of Ephesus had focused on the "proper" activities that are supposed to produce a "dynamic" church but had neglected the most important ingredient.

By man's standards the Ephesian church might seem to be the ideal church. Paul ministered there for about three years and Timothy worked there later on. Scholars believe that the church in Ephesus was so dynamic that it started the other six churches mentioned in Revelation 2 and 3. Jesus, through John, the writer of Revelation, says to this church: "I know your deeds and your toil and perseverance, and that you cannot endure evil men, and you put to the test those who call themselves apostles, and they are not, and you found them to be false; and you have perseverance and have endured for My name's sake, and have not grown weary" (Revelation 2:2-3). He is commending them for what they have done. He is saying: "Your activities are good. You have worked hard for me even to the point of exhaustion. You have been hanging in there when the circumstances have been stacked up against you. On top of all this your spiritual discernment has been outstanding because of the sound doctrine you have embraced." All of this is good, "BUT I have this against you, that you have left your first love" (Revelation 2:4). From a human point of view the Ephesian church had everything going for it, but in the eyes of the Lord Jesus, the Head of the church, there was something woefully lacking.

An interesting comparison can be made between what is said in Revelation about the Ephesian church and the Laodicean church. The church of Laodicea had the same sickness as the Ephesian church only the Laodiceans are described as being in a worse condition. Jesus says to this church: "I know your deeds, that you are neither cold nor hot; I would that you were cold or hot. So because you are lukewarm, and neither hot nor cold, I will spit you out of My mouth" (Revelation 3:15-16). To the Ephesian church Jesus pointed out an underlying problem that had the potential of destroying the church altogether if not arrested. But at Laodicea that same problem had gone farther and had brought them to the very brink of destruction. They were neither cold nor hot, but lukewarm. they were in neutral—coasting along in their lifestyle, but not cultivating a relationship with the Lord. Their lack of a dynamic relationship made Jesus sick enough to vomit.

Later in his message to the Laodiceans Jesus counsels them to become "hot" again—to cultivate a warm relationship with the Lord Himself. He says, "Those whom I love, I reprove and discipline; be zealous therefore, and repent" (Revelation 3:19). He then encourages them to re-open their love relationship with Him: "Behold, I stand at the door and knock; if any one hears My voice and opens the door, I will come in to him, and will dine with him, and he with Me" (Revelation 3:20). He uses a familiar Greek figure of a lover standing at the door of his beloved. This seems to fit very nicely with Christ's words to the Ephesian church that they have "left their first love."

The First Love

It is clear to all believers that Jesus is trying to get a crucial message across. He wants us to return to our first love or, to put it another way, to become "hot" and zealous in our relationship with Him. Notice He does not say that you have lost your first love, but that you have left it or neglected it.

But what is the Christian's first love? Both the message to the Ephesians and that to the Laodiceans have a love theme. As they are compared, it is easy to see that the first love is our reciprocal relationship back to the Lord. It is certain that He loves us. That never changes. Jesus' appeal is for us to reciprocate that love—to cultivate a love relationship with Him.

From "Have-to's" to "Want-to's"

First love is the kind of response many individuals naturally feel toward God as new believers. It's the new believer who freshly appreciates God's love for him. Do you remember how you felt when you realized what had happened to you as a newborn Christian? Remember how you wanted to tell everybody about it, so in your zeal you turned off half of your friends and all of your enemies? You couldn't tell enough people about your new-found relationship. But now you feel you *have* to witness.

Remember how you *wanted* to read your Bible so much that you read everything you could? You started with Genesis (because it was the beginning of the book) and found so many strange people "begetting" one another, killing animals in unusual ways, and then person after person dying. You might have read in 'Ha' bbakuk, Mala'chi, or the Psalms. You really didn't understand, but kept on reading because you *wanted* to. But now you feel you *have* to read your Bible. I marvel at the beautiful innocence of a new believer's prayer. He prays as if God is really there. Those of us who are more "mature" believers pray, "Lord thou knowest that thou hearest as I prayeth." Such language doesn't indicate a genuine relationship with God. I don't talk to real persons like that!

My wife's cousin came to live with us for a time. She was a new believer and made it clear to us during the first 24 hours that she didn't want to pray with us. (She seemed to think mature Christians did that all the time.) Two weeks into her stay she announced that she felt confident enough to pray with us that night. So that evening before going to bed the three of us sat down to pray. We talked over what we were going to pray about and began. When it was her turn to pray she said, "Lord, I just want to pray for . . ."—she had forgotten the guy's name for whom we were praying. She looked up in total desperation and said, "Oh, what's his name?" My first "spiritually mature" response was to think: "You don't stop in the middle of prayer and ask a question of someone else. If you can't think of a person's name, refer to 'him' or make up a name." Then I caught myself and realized how beautiful it was to have that kind of relationship with the Lord.

The first love is that dynamic, reciprocal relationship where the "want-to's" outweigh the "have-to's." The new believer is earnestly desiring to focus on that personal relationship that we were all told about when we received the Lord Jesus as our Savior. Returning to the first love is a rekindling of the warmth of that personal relationship—a cultivation of a love relationship with the Lord Jesus.

Jesus is saying that the works and activities of devotion done by the Ephesian church are good, but there is a dynamic that should take precedence over their deeds, toil, perseverance, and discernment. The first love! It's the beginning, middle, and completion of commitment for a believer. Without this dynamic of the first love, he has absolutely nothing but another stale religion which many people mistakenly call "Christianity." True Christianity is not a religion, but a dynamic, continuing relationship with God through Jesus Christ.

Jesus certainly placed great emphasis upon the reciprocal, first love relationship in His teachings both to believers and non-believers. Matthew records an interesting conversation initiated by a lawyer's question to Jesus:

> "Teacher, which is the great commandment in the Law? And He said to him, 'You shall love the Lord your God with all your heart, and with all your soul, and with all your mind.' This is the great and foremost commandment. And a second is like it, 'you shall love your neighbor as yourself.' On these two commandments depend the whole Law and the Prophets" (Matthew 22:36-40).

Jesus makes it crystal clear that a love relationsnip with God is the most important dynamic ever revealed to mankind.

A Spiritual Bomb

During a meeting with His most devoted followers, Jesus dropped a spiritual "bomb" that is still reverberating around the world. He said, "A new commandment I give to you, that you love one another, even as I have loved you, that you also love one another" (John 13:34). Can you imagine the forcefulness of that statement to the unlikely group of men? I'm sure a few thought, "Jesus, you I love, but do I have to love these other guys, too?" There was the impulsive Peter with a noodle for a backbone and a question mark for a brain. His method of operation was to act first and think later! He's the disciple whose swordsmanship lacked a bit in battle. Instead of bringing his sword down on the soldier's head, he missed and cut off the soldier's ear. "Jesus, you mean we have to love Peter?" Then there was Thomas, the doubter. Every time there was a decision to be made, he was the one who said: "I don't know about this, you guys. I think we had better wait!" The others were tired of his indecisiveness. "Jesus, do we have to love him? If it's up to Thomas, the kingdom will probably be late!"

Another interesting dynamic within the group of disciples was the unlikely relationship between Simon, the

Zealot, and Matthew, the former tax-collector. The Zealots were a bandit group dedicated to defeating the Romans and making life miserable for those Jews who cooperated with the Romans. Matthew was a tax-collector, considered by the Zealots to be traitors—on the side of the Romans.

In a mixture as diverse as this band of followers, Jesus' word seemed like a difficult commandment. Jesus knew this, so a few minutes later He introduced the key ingredient for fulfilling the potentially burdensome command. He says, "If you love me, you will keep My commandments" (John 14:15). Then He says, "He who has My commandments, and keeps them, he it is who loves Me (John 14:21). "If anyone loves Me, he will keep My word" (John 14:23). "He who does not love Me does not keep My words" (John 14:24). Over and over He expresses the same crucial dynamic of a first love relationship with Him.

Fanning the Flame of Love

After Jesus has admonished the Ephesian church for leaving their first love, He delineates how to get back to that relationship. He says, "*Remember* therefore from where you have fallen, and *repent*, and *do* the deeds you did at first" (Revelation 2:5). First, you must remember how it was when you were in that first love relationship—when you were eagerly seeking a personal relationship with the Lord. Second, you must repent—change your mind about your present condition and decide you are going to cultivate that first love. Third, you must do the deeds you did at first. Go back to the basics of the first love relationship no matter how great or little that relationship was. In essence He is saying, "You need to fall in love all over again."

Love Talks

It seems to me that there are at least three essentials involved in falling in love with someone. The same elements are necessary in a love relationship with the Lord Jesus. First you want to *talk* to the one you love. In our counseling center most marital problems are summed up by the patients, "We just can't talk." A normal healthy love relationship must include talking. The same is true of a love relationship with Jesus Christ. You ought to want to talk to the Lord, pray to Him.

Privately

Pray or talk with Him *privately*. Anyone can pray in a group. You can pick up a few key phrases by listening to others, say "Amen" and you've got it! But it's a real test of genuineness to see what you do when you are alone. I had an experience that was one of my most valuable lessons in cultivating my personal relationship with God. It happened years ago when I first started traveling around the country speaking in conferences. I remember vividly one of the first times I was all alone in a hotel room. I was only speaking one hour each for three days. There I was all alone, in a city where no one knew me, and at least ten miles from the conference center. That was one of the toughest battles I've ever faced! It was a personal, hellish struggle against every kind of selfish and wicked thought that had ever entered my mind. "No one would ever know! Besides God's forgiveness is greater than anything I could ever do!" I continued to rationalize my evil fantasies to the point of really wanting to act them out.

Then came the crushing blow! I not only realized afresh how very wicked and self-centered my heart was, but I painfully saw myself as I really was—*another Christian fraud!* A ministerial fraud at that! My mind was directed to the Sermon on the Mount in Matthew 5, 6, and 7, where Jesus specifically contrasted the life of the true believer with the false pharisaical lifestyle. My identification of myself with the Pharisees made me sick!

As I wrestled with the Lord, I reflected all the way back to when I accepted Jesus Christ as my payment for sin, and it all became so beautifully clear. I had been so people- and activity-oriented that I had neglected the very dynamic that makes Christianity Christianity—the cultivation of a personal relationship with Him.

I cried out to the Lord to forgive me for my wasted years with Him when I only checked in on occasion. I learned for the first time to talk with the Lord Jesus as a personal companion throughout the day. I learned the reality of conversing with Him all alone without someone saying, "Let's pray."

Prayer is one of the essential elements of a *personal* relationship with the Lord. It is not meant primarily for public expression, but for private communion with Him (see Chapter III). As valuable as corporate prayer is, there must be a private communication with the Lord in order to cultivate that personal, first love relationship. As Jesus put it, "When you pray, go into your inner room, and when you have shut your door, pray to your Father who is in secret, and your Father who sees in secret will repay you" (Matthew 6:6). Pray privately.

Persistently

Pray *persistently.* The apostle Paul exhorted, "Pray without ceasing" (I Thessalonians 5:17). I remember when I first heard that verse. I thought, "If I were to pray without ceasing, there would be no more basketball, dates, fun, etc.—only prayer!" That would be quite a cramped lifestyle! So I went to my pastor and asked if there was anything in the "original" languages of the Bible that might clarify this verse and solve my dilemma. He pulled out this huge, old book. It was a Greek dictionary. He said, "Oh yes, it really means pray assiduously!" I nodded my head as if I knew what that meant, rushed home to look that up and found that it meant "persistently." We are to pray persistently!

There was a little boy named Johnny. He was only five years old. One day he went to his dad and said, "Dad, I want a baby brother. What can I do to help?" He had heard some talk around the house about the possibility of a new "little bundle" coming soon. His dad was very perceptive and viewed this as an opportunity to teach Johnny about prayer. So he said: "I'll tell you what. If you'll start praying that God will give you a baby brother, I guarantee you that you'll have a baby brother in just two months!" (Obviously, Dad knew something that Johnny didn't know.) So Johnny responded to the challenge by going to his bedroom early that night and praying that God would give him a baby brother.

Johnny prayed every night for one month, but was becoming skeptical. He had checked around the neighborhood and found out that this kind of thing had never happened in the history of the neighborhood. You just don't pray for two months and then, Whamo!—a new baby appears. So Johnny quit praying! At the end of two months Johnny's mother went to the hospital. When she came back home, the parents called Johnny into the bedroom to surprise him with his answer to prayer. Johnny walked cautiously into the room, not expecting to find anything. But there was a little bundle lying right next to his mother. Dad pulled the blanket back and there were twins—two baby brothers. Johnny's dad looked down at Johnny and said, "Now aren't you glad you prayed?" Johnny looked back up at his dad and said, "Yes, but aren't you glad I quit when I did?"

Well, Johnny blew it! He was doing so well—praying persistently. But really, many believers do the same thing as little Johnny. They start praying earnestly and persistently for something, but then they check around the neighborhood and someone out there says, "Oh, God doesn't do that kind of thing; what you're praying for is impossible." Intimidated by the "neighborhood" they quit praying. Persistent prayer is praying for something until you get sufficient peace about the matter so that you can act, stop acting, or leave the matter with Him.

Specifically

Pray *specifically*. We tend to pray too generally. "Heal the sick." "Raise the dead." A common general prayer is

"Bless this meeting." Now what would you like God to do? I'm convinced that if it were possible the Lord might be confused about what we want, because we are confused about what we're asking. After hearing some prayers (mine included) I can almost hear a questioning response vibrating from heaven saying "HUH???" It would be interesting to be able to listen in on the prayer lines that go back and forth from earth to heaven and back to earth again. On the earthly line you might hear, "Lord, I just want to pray for John tonight." The heavenly response, "What about him?" "I just wanted to mention his name to you." Or, "Please help Mary." "Help Mary what?"

When I was in the third grade, I prayed, "Lord, bless the missionaries in Africa." My Sunday School teacher came up after class to straighten me out. She explained that I was praying in generalities. She said, "What do you want God to do for the missionaries in Africa?" I didn't know! Then she asked, "How would you know if they ever got blessed?" I just figured that they would write their monthly missionary letter and would say that in the month of February they were blessed. I hadn't thought about it. I took my teacher's comments to heart and was prepared for the next Sunday School class, because I knew she would ask me to pray again just to see if I had learned her mini-lesson on prayer. Sure enough she called on me at the end of the class and I prayed, "Lord, bless the missionaries in South Africa!" (At least it was more specific than before!)

We must learn to pray more specifically, so that we can know when God answers one of our petitions. Many have found it helpful to write down specific requests on a pad. Whatever method of prayer you try, consciously work at particularizing your prayers. One young coed got down to the basic particulars when she prayed, "Lord, I'm not asking for myself, but please send my mother a son-in-law!" Now, that's specific prayer!

Love Listens

So in cultivating a personal first love relationship with the Lord you ought to want to talk to Him. The second essential element is that you ought to want to *listen* to Him. Talking to the Lord is through prayer and listening is primarily through His revealed Word—the Bible.

"Hit and Miss" Method

For years I used the most popular method of listening to God's Word. It may be called the "hit-and-miss" method. You take your Bible (any version will do) in the left hand. You then point· your right index finger toward heaven (in the one-way tradition). Slowly bring that index finger toward the page's edge. Then when you feel so moved, thrust your spiritually prepared finger into the pages of the Bible and read the passage of the day. Sounds exciting, but it's absolutely devastating!

A funny story is told of one man who used the hit-and-miss method. His holy finger happened to land on the verse, "And Judas went out and hanged himself!" That's nothing to meditate on throughout the day, so he tried again. On his second attempt, he landed on, "Go thou and do likewise!" Now it's getting worse, instead of better. He tried a third time and it said, "What thou doest, do quickly!" Now that is certainly a fictitious story, but there are many people who are hanging at the end of a spiritual rope because they *can't* get into the Bible and listen to the Lord. Let's change that verb from *can't* to *won't!* In most cases it's a simple matter of a decision of the will.

With all of the bombardment of counterfeit information today, it's a must to cultivate a personal relationship with the Lord through the only genuine source—His revelation. The best defense against the counterfeit is to know the genuine very well.

Love Pleases

The final essential element in cultivating a love relationship with the Lord Jesus is that you want to *please* Him. When cultivating a human love relationship, you want to please the object loved in any way you can. When I was a junior in high school, I thought I was in love with a certain girl (*thought* I was). For Christmas I pulled out all of the stops and bought her a beautiful (and expensive) sweater. There we were exchanging gifts on Christmas Eve. I knew she would be ecstatic about her sweater. She opened her gift first. She was overwhelmed just as I had hoped! Then it was my turn to open her gift to me. Of course, it's just the thought that counts. And I must admit, I had lots of thoughts going through my mind when I saw it. She gave me a sweater, too. But it wasn't a normal sweater. It was about 31 shades of brown! I'd never seen anything like it in my life! It looked like two roaches had knitted it together. Sometimes when I had it on, I thought they were still knitting, it was so scratchy! Can you guess what I did with it? (I'm embarrassed to tell you.) I wore it! Every time I thought she would be around, I wore it. *I wore* that sweater!!! I wore that sweater because I thought I was in love with her. When you are in love with someone, you want to please him/her.

The same is true in our relationship with the Lord Jesus. The first love relationship is cultivated by pleasing Him. The interesting thing is that the more you build that personal relationship by pleasing Him, the more you are motivated to please Him, because of the dynamic of the love relationship. Loving Him and pleasing Him go hand-in-hand, as Jesus said, "If you love Me, you will keep My commandments" (John 14:15). The commandments of a religion are heavy, but the commandments of a love relationship are not burdensome.

Wouldn't you like to cultivate that personal first love relationship with the Lord? It's the dynamic around which everything else must revolve. Without that love relationship, you have absolutely nothing—nothing but another religion!

Do You Love Me?

In the last chapter of the Gospel of John an intriguing conversation between Jesus and Peter occurs. It is the third time Jesus has appeared to them since His death and resurrection and it seems to be the most extensive time of the three. The disciples were out in the boat fishing about 100 yards from shore. They had caught nothing all night. At approximately daybreak Jesus appeared on the beach and called to the men to see if they had caught any fish. When they answered in the negative, He told them to throw their net to the other side. After that they caught so many fish that they were unable to haul them into the boat. They realized because of the "supernatural fishing trip" that it was Jesus who was standing on the shore. Naturally, Peter was unwilling to wait to row to shore with the others, so he tried his walk-on-water trick once more. It didn't work! He had to swim.

Finally, everyone made it to shore. Apparently Jesus had already built a fire. While they were cooking and eating the fish, very little was said. I think there is very good reason for that. Peter must have still felt the guilt from denying the Lord in the exact manner the Lord prophesied. You know how you feel when you are about to be confronted by someone about an area of guilt. Stomach moves to throat. Choking begins. No doubt Peter was seated next to Jesus just waiting for Him to drop the bomb and say, "I told you so."

After much apprehensive silence, the feared time of confrontation came. Jesus leaned toward Peter. (Stomach moves to throat. Choking begins.) He said, "Peter, do you love Me more than these?" I'm convinced Peter was happily shocked by the question. He was expecting anything but that.

He quickly retorted, "Yes, Lord; You know that I love You."
Jesus said to him, "Tend My lambs." Jesus knew that Peter
did not understand fully the question He had posed, so He
asked him again a second time, "Simon, do you love Me?"
Peter again responded with, "Yes, Lord; You know that I love
You." Jesus said to him, "Shepherd My sheep." Jesus came
right back the third time and asked, "Simon, do you love
Me?" Peter was grieved because He asked the question the
third time and he said to Him, "Lord, You know all things;
You know that I love You." Jesus said to him, "Tend My
sheep."

With Peter under a heavy "guilt pile," you might think
that Jesus' approach would be to get a confession, or to move
Peter toward an attitude of repentance. But instead Jesus goes
directly to the heart of the matter. Even in the case of one who
is overwhelmed with the personal guilt of denying the Savior,
Jesus was not concerned with his sin, his guilt, his prayer life,
his knowledge of the Word, whether he has been spirit-filled
or has experienced the baptism of the Holy Spirit. Jesus was
primarily concerned with Peter's dynamic first love relationship with his Lord.

Jesus asked Peter the most basic question any believer
could be asked. It's the bottom-line question for the Christian
life. "Do you love me? If so, then act like it!" For without the
first love relationship with Jesus Christ there can be no action
which merits anyone's attention. Without that dynamic relationship there is no Christian lifestyle. The Lord Jesus is asking the same question of you and me right now: "Do you love
me?" "Do you love me?" "Do you love me?" True Christianity is not a religion, but a love relationship with God
through Jesus Christ. *Anything short of a demonstration of
that relationship between the holy God of the universe and
sinful man cannot and must not be called Christianity.*

Two

THE VERTICAL RELATIONSHIP IN FOCUS

If you were asked to draw a stick-figure picture of a happy believer, what would you draw? A great big grin with a person behind it? One person sharing the Four Spiritual Laws with another? A person kneeling in prayer with his hands clasped under his chin? A smiling person with a ten-pound black Holy Bible tucked under his arm? A family entering the doors of the First Bapterian Church? If you would draw any one of the above, you would be wrong!

Our tendency is to focus on the externals rather than on what is going on inside a person. It's because of this tendency that when we try to use our spiritual thermometers on a person we come up with the wrong temperature. "How's Bob doing?" "He's doing very well. I saw him in church again last night." Sure, Bob's body may have been sitting in the pew, but Bob may have been dying inside.

Not only do we view other people through the wrong lens, but we tend to make the same mistake in analyzing our own actions as a believer. As long as we are doing the "right" things and going to the "right" meetings, we believe we are spiritually healthy. Everything seems to work very well until our spiritual routine is interrupted by a crisis or because of a variety of other reasons we are unable to "perform." At this point there is usually an emotional crash, which ranges from a mood of disappointment to deep depression. Regardless of how dramatic the crash is or how fast a person is able to bounce back, the vertical relationship with the Lord is out of focus. This vertical relationship with the Lord does not emphasize "doing" as much as "being." Who you are and what you are becoming is more important than what you are doing. When the "doing" is given more importance than the "being," a certain *religious lifestyle* dominates our view of Christianity. "Man looks at the outward appearance [doing], but the Lord looks at the heart [being]" (I Samuel 16:7).

The Happy Believer

When Jesus addressed Himself to the question "What is a happy believer?" He focused on the "being" behind the "doing." The components that produce a happy believer as Jesus describes him are quite different from those normally suggested. He goes directly to the heart!

Early in His ministry Jesus made it clear that He had come to bring a new focus to the believer's lifestyle. His focus is both vertical and horizontal as He describes it in what is probably the most profound lecture of all time—the Beatitudes! He uses the term "blessed" in all eight frames of His composite picture of a happy, healthy believer. "Blessed" means happy, or to be congratulated. Jesus is referring to a "gut-level" joy in a person's innermost being. The first four beatitudes speak of our vertical relationship with the Lord (our "being"). The second four speak of our horizontal relationships with others (our "doing").

The Vertical Principles

A happy believer has a good self-image. He knows who he is before God and who he is before others. A person has a healthy view of himself when he knows who he is and lives accordingly. However, such self-esteem cannot be developed in a vacuum. It must take place within the context of relationships. Each relationship is like a mirror from which a person receives reflections of himself. The Christian lifestyle involves two types of mirrors—the vertical and the horizontal. Let's put the vertical relationship in focus by examining the first four beatitudes.

Poor in Spirit

"Blessed are the poor in spirit, for theirs is the kingdom of heaven."

What does "poor in spirit" mean? When I first encountered this phrase, I tried to avoid it. It seemed to me to mean more poverty, and I was poor enough! I didn't need that. The imagery here is of a beggar who must beg for his very survival. He's that poor. But this phrase doesn't refer to material poverty. It speaks of an immaterial poverty—pride poverty. It's the opposite of a "haughty spirit." It's anti-pride! Jesus seems to be speaking of a sense of inadequacy. Happy is the man who has a sense of inadequacy? Exactly! A sense of inadequacy before God, a right evaluation of yourself before the Lord. Being "poor in spirit" means coming to the realization that before the holy God of the universe you are absolutely nothing and can do nothing to please Him. That's because of the evil and self-centered nature that is so much a part of you, what many refer to as the old sin nature—the wickedness of man.

Now just because you are *nothing* doesn't mean that you are a *nobody!* Some people misinterpret this nothing idea and begin praying, "Lord, make me nothing!" I had a professor in seminary who said, "Take it by faith, you already are!" Although man is totally wicked in his nature, he is not for that reason worthless. This is because of the wonder of man's origin—created in the image of God. There is something special about him. He is not a plant or an animal. Man is created in God's image. There is something basically valuable about man because of this fact. For the believer there is an additional aspect to his value as a person—the fact of his new creation in Christ. Happy is the man who has a right evaluation of himself before God—his wickedness and his wonder.

The second beatitude picks right up on the concept of the first.

Mourn

"Blessed are those who mourn, for they shall be comforted."
Blessed are those who mourn? How can happiness be harmonized with mourning? Jesus introduced this same idea to the disciples in their last meeting together. After announcing that He would soon depart out of this world, He said: "You will *weep* and *lament*, but the world will rejoice; you will be *sorrowful*, but your sorrow will be turned to joy. Whenever a woman is in travail she has sorrow, because her hour has come; but when she gives birth to the child, she remembers the anguish no more, for joy that a child has been born into the world. Therefore you, too, now have sorrow; but I will see you again, and your heart will rejoice" (John 16:20-22). His disciples were going to be weeping and lamenting over the fact of His departure. They would not be near to the God-man for a while. Their "mourning" would be the result of their separation from the Lord. It's interesting to note that Jesus discussed this in the same context where He promised to send another Comforter. "Blessed are those who mourn, for they shall be comforted."

Paul picks up this theme of mourning and lamenting in his second letter to the Corinthians. He describes a believer as an "earthen vessel" (temporal) which has a heavenly "treasure" dwelling within" (II Corinthians 4:7). The old sinful body (the "earthly house") keeps us from experiencing fully the heavenly treasure (our new creation). He says: "For we know that if the earthly tent which is our house is torn down, we have a building from God, a house not made with hands, eternal in the heavens. For indeed in this house we *groan*, longing to be clothed with our dwelling from heaven; inasmuch as we, having put it on, shall not be found naked.

For indeed while we are in this tent, we groan, being burdened, because we do not want to be unclothed, but to be clothed, in order that what is mortal may be swallowed up by life" (II Corinthians 5:1-4). Again, there is the theme of mourning, groaning over the separation a believer senses from the total, perfect experience of being in union with God.

James speaks of the same thing in his letter. To the rich he says: "*Weep* and *howl* for your miseries which are coming upon you. Your riches have rotted and your garments have become moth-eaten. Your gold and your silver have rusted; and their rust will be a witness against you. . . . Behold, the pay of the laborers who mowed your fields, and which has been withheld by you, cries out against you; and the outcry of those who did the harvesting has reached the ears of the Lord. . . . You have lived luxuriously on the earth . . ." (James 5:1-5). He is exhorting the rich, who have trusted in their riches and misused their wealth to the point of mistreating people to "mourn"—weep and howl. In another passage James instructs those who are lifted up with pride: "Draw near to God and He will draw near to you. Cleanse your hands, you sinners; and purify your hearts, you double-minded. Be *miserable* and *mourn* and *weep* . . ." (James 4:8-9).

Mourn over what? In each of these instances—weeping, lamenting, groaning and sorrowing—it is *mourning over that which keeps a person from God*. To the disciples, it was remaining behind in this world without Jesus next to them. To the Corinthians, it was the "earthly house" filled with sin and inadequacies that kept them from enjoying the heavenly "treasure" of God within them. To the rich, their wealth and power separated them from experiencing God's true wealth and power. To the proud, it was the prideful spirit of their hearts that kept them from enjoying true exaltation in God's grace. So what is mourning? Mourning seems to be a sensitivity to that which keeps a person from God. That which might keep you from God may come from within—the wickedness of the old sin nature—or from without—the world-system with all its decay and Satan with all his evil schemings. (This source of adversity will be discussed more fully in "Where in the World Is the Devil?")

Applying the principle of mourning is one of the most valuable steps in rebuilding a good, healthy self-image. Many times when a believer sins, he becomes deeply depressed. Quite often when this occurs, he falls into at least two traps. The first is shock over the fact that he sinned. Why should a person be shocked about that? Because of the sin nature wickedness dwells within a believer, and that dirty, old, lustful sin nature renders the believer capable of doing almost anything, any place, any time. So why the shock?

There is an interesting phrase commonly used in the pulpit which, although it may be expressed with good intentions, mistakenly implies that believers can be free from the presence of sin in their lives. The question is asked, "Do you have any known sin in your life?" The "correct" and "spiritual" answer is expected to be No. But when I am asked that question, my answer is Yes. Do I ever! In John's first letter he makes this clear: "If we say that we have no sin, we are deceiving ourselves, and the truth is not in us. If we confess our sins, He is faithful and righteous to forgive us our sins and to cleanse us from all unrighteousness. If we say that we have not sinned, we make Him a liar, and His word is not in us" (I - John 1:8-10). You should not be at all shocked to rediscover that you sin. To deny that you have sin dwelling in your body or to believe that you can attain any form of sinless perfection (no matter how temporary) is nothing but self-deception. In a very real sense such shock reflects a spirit of pride. "I'm shocked that *I* could have done that!" But why not you? What makes anyone exempt from blowing it at a given moment? Absolutely nothing! Pride may manifest itself in either of two ways—a sense of inferiority or of superiority! Pride shown by inferiority is thinking that you ought to be better or deserve better. Pride shown by superiority is thinking that you *are* better. (These two dimensions will be discussed further in "People Who Need People").

The second trap a believer may slip into when he sins is that of mourning over the wrong thing. It is the individual who sins. You are responsible for your action of yielding to the allurement of the flesh (old sin nature), the world system and its values, the temptations of the Devil. You can never say, "The Devil made me do it!"

However, your mourning should not consist of beating yourself down because of your sin. When you do that, you are just trying to pay for the sin by yourself. The sin has been paid for by the death of Jesus on the cross. In order for you to appropriate that payment at any given moment (forgiveness), you must only acknowledge (confess) that your sin is an offense against God. The Bible does not say that you are to cry and lament and mourn for the forgiveness of your sin. Person after person walks into our counseling center suffering because of this trap. They hate themselves for doing something wrong or for not doing something they should have done.

Mourning is not hating yourself, but hating that which keeps you from God. I don't hate myself. As a matter of fact, I really like myself! So when I sin, I accept the responsibility for my sin and acknowledge it as sin against God. I don't blame my sin nature, the world, or the Devil for it, but I mourn over that which encourages me to sin or causes me to stumble. I am not my own enemy. That which keeps me from God is my enemy; that which is out to separate me from my supernatural relationship with Him. I mourn over the fact that I have a sin nature (a magnet within) attracted away from God, that I live in a world-system (a magnet on the outside) pulling me away from God, and the Devil in between bringing the two magnets together. I hate those compelling forces! "Happy are those who mourn."

Woe is Me

The best illustration of the first two beatitudes ("poor in spirit" and "mourning") working together is the experience of Isaiah's vision. Isaiah, the Jewish prophet, relates his vision this way: "In the year of King Uzziah's death, I saw the Lord sitting on a throne, lofty and exalted, with the train of His robe filling the temple. Seraphim stood above Him, each having six wings; with two he covered his face, and with two he covered his feet, and with two he flew. And one called out to another and said, 'Holy, Holy, Holy, is the Lord of hosts, the whole earth is full of His glory.' And the foundations of the thresholds trembled at the voice of Him who called out, while the temple was filling with smoke. Then I said, 'Woe is me, for I am ruined! Because I am a man of unclean lips, and I live among a people of unclean lips; for my eyes have seen the King, the Lord of hosts' " (Isaiah 6:1-5).

First of all Isaiah saw God in all of His holiness and glory, and in light of this he saw himself in all of his sinfulness. It was only after viewing God's holiness that he was able to see clearly his "unclean lips" and the "unclean lips" of the world around him. Isaiah's entire existence was being placed into proper perspective before the Lord. He was poor in spirit—he saw himself as he really was before God. He then mourned over the "unclean lips" of the people and his own uncleanness—both of which kept him from God.

It's interesting to note the next scene in Isaiah's vision, "Then one of the seraphim flew to me, with a burning coal in his hand which he had taken from the altar with tongs. And he touched my mouth with it and said, 'Behold, this has touched your lips; and your iniquity is taken away, and your sin is forgiven.' Then I heard the voice of the Lord, saying, 'Whom shall I send, and who will go for us?' Then I said, 'Here am I. Send me!'" (Isaiah 6:6-8). Here is a beautiful picture of a man who was filthy dirty before the holy God, saw himself as he really was (poor in spirit), and mourned over that which kept him from God. Notice though that after being forgiven he did not continue to lament and groan about all that he had done wrong. On the contrary, when the next spiritual commission came up, he eagerly and confidently volunteered for it: "Here am I. Send me!" Does this sound like a man who was down on himself? Hardly! He was a man who mourned over that which kept him from enjoying his relationship with the Lord. Then he accepted forgiveness and began to enjoy God again. "Happy are those who mourn."

Meek

"Blessed are the meek, for they shall inherit the earth."

Poor in spirit is a person's right evaluation of himself before God in light of his wickedness (sin nature) and the wonder of who he is (in the image of God). Mourning focuses on how to deal with the wickedness—that which man has going *against* him. Meekness is concerned with the wonder of man—that which man has going *for* him.

Meekness is not weakness! It's a strength that evidences self-control. Meekness is not passive. It's a response based on the strength and confidence derived from a relationship with the God of the universe. Jesus illustrates this beatitude when He speaks of turning the other cheek to an anonymous hand that comes out of the darkness and slaps a person. Jesus doesn't give the identity of the aggressor. He doesn't seem to care. What does concern Jesus is, "What are you going to do with the other side of your face?" His instruction to the happy believer is to turn the other cheek and invite the aggressor to bruise that side as well. But why? Because as a believer who has a relationship with the God of the universe you do not need to react in this situation. The attacker has a much deeper problem than you will ever have, so your reaction is to be a quiet, controlled confidence in your wonder. You are created in the image of God and, as a believer, are a new creation in Him. That counts for a lot more than any bruised face. Meekness views life from the eternal perspective, and is confident and strong because of it.

These first three beatitudes speak basically of our inadequacy and God's sufficiency. Naturally, where we lack is predominant in this comparison. To dwell on our lacking could be extremely negative and would certainly not be very encouraging. The fourth beatitude shifts gears somewhat and tells us what to do in order to fill up what we lack.

Hungry and Thirsty for Righteousness

"Blessed are those who hunger and thirst for righteousness, for they shall be satisfied."

Those who hunger and thirst for righteousness will be happy, because they will be filled up where they have lacked. The term "satisfied" was used of fattening up cattle and meant to fill them up until they want no more. This beatitude is not some kind of pious platitude. In fact, it may be one of the most powerful promises in the Bible. A satisfied lifestyle! How do you experience it? By hungering and thirsting after righteousness.

As you trace the word "righteousness" through the Bible you will find that it refers to God's standard of right and wrong. Believers are *affirmed righteous* in Christ and then are encouraged to act righteously in their lifestyle. The latter emphasis seems to be what Jesus had in mind here. To act righteously is to walk in a manner that is consistent with God's standard. Jesus walked consistently with God's standard, therefore He is referred to as the Righteous One. So then, it is those who hunger and thirst to walk according to God's standard—to be like Christ—who are promised happiness.

Why do you think Jesus used the terms hunger and thirst? I think it's because the Lord knew what my natural response would be. When I first started digging into the Sermon on the Mount, I decided to go through the Beatitudes verse by verse and ask myself how they might be applied. When I reached the fourth one, I asked, "Am I hungering and thirsting for righteousness?" My immediate response was, "Well, I really desire to be Christlike." But that wasn't the question. "Am I hungering and thirsting after it?" Again I came back with, "It's definitely one of my top priorities!" Then it hit me. Hungering and thirsting! These are terms of necessity and therefore require action. There is spiritual necessity in the sense that without the righteous lifestyle there will be no satisfaction. It's absolutely necessary to hunger and thirst. Hunger and thirst are terms of action as well. I'm known as a "Tab-aholic"—I really like Tab! It doesn't make any difference how much it costs or what kind of effort needs to be expended to get it. When I'm thirsty for a Tab, I go get it! Jesus is saying, "Happy are those who are hungering and thirsting enough to do something about it, enough to walk consistently with God's standard." Are you hungering and thirsting?

The phrase hunger and thirst also strongly implies that a process is involved. Jesus is not offering a push-button, instant breakfast approach to Christlikeness. He is not speaking of a one-time decision to hunger and thirst for righteousness. It's a process of growth and maturity.

The Vertical Process

Although more will be said later concerning the process of living the Christian lifestyle (Part Two), it's important here to discuss how the principle of process is related to the believer's vertical relationship with God. There are many passages in the Bible that outline progressive steps in the process of maturity. In John 15 Jesus thoroughly discusses with his disciples the matter of relationships. These relationships are to the Lord, to other believers, and to the world. In each type of relationship He sets forth what our responsibility should be.

The first relationship He discusses is that between the believer and his Lord. The believer is commanded to abide in Christ as a branch abides in the vine. This abiding is a confident, dependent commitment to the Lord. Then Jesus says, "If you abide in Me, and My words abide in you, ask whatever you wish, and it shall be done for you" (John 15:7). There are both active and passive dimensions to this relationship. The active is obviously our commitment to abide in Him, but the passive is easily skipped over—"My words abide in you." There is more to the dynamic, vertical relationship with the Lord than a simple commitment to Him. There is also some kind of taking-in of the Word so that it acts upon my life.

Offer Your Body

In Romans, Chapter 12, Paul discusses the process of maturity in an extensive way and comes to similar conclusions as Jesus does in John 15. He says, "I urge you, therefore, brethren, by the mercies of God, to present your bodies a living and holy sacrifice, acceptable to God, which is your spiritual service of worship" (Romans 12:1). In this verse Paul is urging us to offer our bodies to God for service. He is appealing to what God has done for us as a motivating force, "by the mercies of God," and he's calling for that same commitment to abide in the Lord that was mentioned in John 15. That, again, is the active dimension.

As a young person I heard more sermons and sermonettes on this verse than on any other, and I responded to it as I was instructed. I walked down the center aisle during the "altar call." I threw sticks in the campfire as a symbol of my commitment. I stood at calls for dedication and commitment. I wrote out "sin lists" and watched them burn in the fire. I stood on hymn books. I even tried the side aisles. I mean to tell you, I tried it all! I once counted 43 times that I made this commitment to offer my body to God. I finally gave up. There just wasn't any consistency to it all. Besides, I was tired of all of the dramatic antics.

Overhaul your Mind

After much frustration and disappointment, I realized what had been wrong. I had made the most common mistake in biblical interpretation and application—I didn't read far enough. After 1 comes 2. Verse 2 says, "*And* do not be conformed to this world, but be transformed by the renewing of your mind, that you may prove what the will of God is, that which is good and acceptable and perfect" (Romans 12:2). This is the passive (where something acts upon me) dimension which corresponds with the John 15:7 phrase—"My words abide in you." Paul says not to be fit into the mold of the world (conformed), but to be "transformed," totally changed inside out by the renewing of your mind. That was it! For me to progress in the process of maturity I not only needed to *offer my body to God*, but also *allow my mind to be overhauled* by the Word of God.

The world-system is a vast battlefront for the minds of men and women. From the moment of birth, we are continually being programmed by principles and values that teach us how to live for ourselves without God. The best way to counteract this programming by the world-system is to re-program your mind with the living Word of God.

Not You in the Word—But the Word into You!

Reprogramming the mind does not so much involve your getting into the Word—though this is necessary—as it involves getting the Word into you. The Bible is saturated with promises about meditation, allowing the "live and powerful" Word to abide in you. The Lord makes many promises concerning its effect on our lives: prosperity and success (Joshua 1:8), fruitfulness and abundance (Psalm 1:2-3), deliverance from sin (Psalm 119:9, 11), wisdom (Psalm 119:97, 100), answered prayer (John 15:7), power over the Devil (I John 2:14), etc.

It sounded great to me! (Sure beats walking down long church aisles or hunting for sticks of rededication.) So I began re-programming my mind. I started with the first chapter of James where it says, "Consider it all joy, my brethren, when you encounter various trials; knowing that the testing of your faith produces endurance" (James 1:2-3). At the same time I turned all my possessions over to the Lord. I had done this before, but I felt that I wanted a fresh start as I began my new project. These possessions included my beautiful new blue car (a Buick Skylark!). It was the only thing I owned that was really difficult to give over to the Lord, and I was extremely

protective about it. Whenever my wife would return after having used the car I would immediately check it out to look for
any scratches. The blue Skylark had definitely become a problem in my life, so I gave it to the Lord and thanked Him for
the privilege of using it. It was God's car!

God's Car—Crunched

That first week of meditating was super. I enjoyed it, and
I was excited about continuing. During the second week my
wife and I were to pick up some friends at the airport. We met
them at the gate and packed their luggage in the trunk. Before
I could start my car, I noticed that a red Corvette was backing
up right toward my door. I thought, "He'll certainly stop!"
Well, he did, but only after the door on my side had helped
him. Normally, my reaction would have been a bit explosive,
but something incredible had happened to me. The verse
from James 1 came before my mind: "Consider it all joy, my
brethren, when you encounter various trials . . ."—signed,
God! I didn't have a choice. I got out of my car (from the pas-
senger side) and was greeted by the driver of the Corvette,
who was now shouting and screaming at *me!* (I hadn't even
turned my engine on.) We went casually on our way after
settling with the man, but I realized that I was a changed person. I couldn't believe how I had reacted to that small crisis. I
liked it!

God's Car—Scratched

The next week we went on a camping trip up the California coast. We took God's car (my former car) and fastened a
luggage carrier on the roof for all our paraphernalia. When we
arrived at our first campsite, my friend, Dick, started to un-
load the carrier. As he pulled the tent out of the carrier, the
charcoal grill came along with it. As it made its way down to
the ground, it made a beautiful artistic design on the right

hand door of my new, blue, Buick Skylark. I was standing about ten feet away watching the whole tragedy take place. Normally, my reaction would have been to slip into an infuriated state—but that just didn't happen! At the precise moment when I was about to react "normally," that passage from James lit up in my mind: "Consider it all joy, my brethren, when you encounter various trials . . ." Again, it was signed, God! There was no doubt that this was another of the "various" trials! So I found myself saying, "O.K., God, I count it all joy, but you sure don't take very good care of your car!" More important than what I said was the way I felt deep inside on the gut level. I was actually freed from the anxiety that would have been my normal reaction. Again I was shocked by the change, but I liked it. I was beginning to realize the power of meditating on the Word of God.

God's Car—Crinkled

After learning the lesson of counting it all joy, I enthusiastically moved on to other passages that identified weaknesses in my thoughts, actions, and reactions. I didn't know that I was in for a couple of refresher courses about James. Two months later I was driving to the seminary campus one morning to pick up my mail. I was in the left hand lane of a one-way street, and a man in the right lane decided he was going to make a left hand turn. He was going to have to go through me to do it, and he did! He turned left and crashed into my right, back fender. This time I started to react. I stopped and angrily jumped out of my car. But before I could get to him that same sign flashed in my mind. When I acknowledged the reception of the message and agreed with God about it, I was released from my anger.

God's Car—Smashed

Later that day I was to meet a friend downtown at his office. It was raining a little and the streets were quite slippery. I was stopped at one of the on-ramps of the main expressway in the city waiting for the car in front of me to go. Finally, there was a break in the traffic and he went on. I moved into position, saw that no one was coming, and darted out onto the expressway—at least that was my intention! As I accelerated toward the freeway I was looking back for any more traffic. The next thing I knew I had hit something very hard. I couldn't imagine what it was, and I couldn't see what it was because the hood of my car was standing straight up!

I got out of my car and realized what had happened. The man in front of me was an international student at the local university. He wasn't used to driving on the slick streets with his big new car, and when he took off his wheels started spinning. That scared him and so he stopped right in the middle of the on-ramp. He was moaning and groaning in some other language and holding his neck in pain. I couldn't believe what a mess I was in—two times in one day. I thought my course on trials was over, but I found that I had been enrolled in "Remedial Trials 103"!

A policeman arrived at the scene. He asked, "Is that your car?" (I didn't have the nerve to tell him that it really belonged to God. I'm sure if I had, he would have given me a test for intoxication.) I answered, "Yeah, that's my car—the blue one with the hood standing straight up!" After gathering all of the pertinent information, the officer helped me tie my hood down so that I could drive it. I cautiously drove home thinking over the advantages of riding a bicycle or taking the bus instead of owning a car. I parked the car carefully so my wife could enjoy a full view of the accumulated damage to "God's" car from our 4th floor apartment. There it was; a beautiful blue Buick Skylark with a caved-in left front door, an artistic design on the right front door, a smashed right back fender, and a bowed and wrinkled hood tied down with wire. Her comment was classic: "You're still learning, huh?"

How the Mind Can Be Renewed

The process of renewing the mind takes time. I don't

know of anything that has been more difficult for me than meditation, and yet I don't know of anything that has been more profitable and life-changing for me. It's the continual process of allowing the Word of God to "abide in you." Let me suggest a way to do this.

Step 1 is *intensive observation*. Select a passage, at least a paragraph, that speaks to a problem or concern you are having. Go over, preferably memorizing, the passage until you really know it—feed your mind on the principles contained in it! The important thing to remember is that you cannot observe too much. The more you look, the more you see!

Step 2 is *honest evaluation*. Make a list of areas of weakness where your life does not match up to the selected passage. For example in I Corinthians 13 you may read that love is not jealous. Ask yourself, "Am I jealous?" (For most of us, a better question is "When am I jealous?") If you are, then write out the contexts in which you feel jealousy. Be honest and specific. You will find that you are listing ways in which you want to grow to be like the Lord Jesus—His thoughts, actions, and reactions.

Step 3 is *thorough personalization*. Run the passage through your mind over and over. Then pray, "Lord, whatever you have to do, work this quality into my life, because I want to be more like Your Son." That is a dangerous thing to pray unless you really mean it! The Lord is always looking for a believer whose heart is open to be changed into qualities of Christlikeness. He seems to send an angel "air mail special delivery" when we express that kind of attitude. In this step you must seek to apply the passage. Look for promises to claim, commands to obey or sins to acknowledge. Ask yourself the question "What does this passage tell me to do?"

This particular method of renewing your mind is just a *suggestion*. Use it, adapt it, or throw it out, but whatever you do RENEW YOUR MIND! There is no better way to become more like the Living Word, Christ, than to renew your mind through His Word. And there is no better way to bring the *vertical relationship into focus* than to renew your mind!

Vertical Preservative—Salt!

Immediately following the Beatitudes Jesus seems to condense the vertical relationship (poor in spirit, mourn, meek, hunger and thirst for righteousness; into one word—*salt*. He says, "You are the salt of the earth; but if the salt has become tasteless, how will it be made salty again? It is good for nothing anymore except to be thrown out and trampled under foot by men" (Matthew 5:13). He is not speaking of salt as a food to make something tasty or to make someone thirsty. Salt was a preservative. It was used primarily to preserve foods from decaying. If salt becomes unsalty or ineffective ("tasteless"), it is useful for nothing and will have to be thrown away. This is a statement of practical impossibility. It's unthinkable that salt would become unsalty or non-salt!

Jesus applied this term to believers, saying that believers are to be the salt of the earth—*the preservative in view of the world's decay!* Salt represents a quality of relationship with the heavenly Father that has a preserving effect on the world. Although believers may choose not to have that quality of relationship with God, and therefore have no preserving effect on the world, the potential for preserving is always present for salt cannot become non-salt. Salt is the "being" dimension of the Christian lifestyle. As we will see throughout the book, it's *the vertical relationship in focus!*

Three

THE HORIZONTAL RELATIONSHIP IN FOCUS

Whereas the first four beatitudes bring into focus our vertical relationship, the second four bring the horizontal relationship into focus—our dealings with people before the Lord. The focus is more on the "doing," but it's very clear that there can be no quality "doing" without quality "being"—no healthy horizontal relationship without a healthy vertical relationship. Even though we have come to the dimension of "doing," the emphasis is still on the internal quality behind any particular action toward others.

The Horizontal Principles

Merciful

"Blessed are the merciful, for they shall receive mercy."

Happy is the person who demonstrates compassion to others. Showing mercy or demonstrating compassion is seeing someone in need and trying to meet that need through your own resources. It grows out of empathy for another's problem or need. It may be shown by providing a listening ear when someone just needs to talk. It may be comforting a person during time of sorrow. It may be sharing what you have (money, possessions, yourself) with someone who needs just that. It may be having compassion for a friend who doesn't have a personal relationship with the Lord.

When I was in high school, I was filled with compassion for my friends concerning their relationship with God, but I didn't know what to say or do. Consequently, I turned off half of my friends and all of my enemies with my misguided compassion. (The process of the common "turn-off" will be discussed later in Part Three.) Once on my way to school I prayed that God would give me an opportunity to talk to one of my friends that day. At first period study hall my good friend sat next to me and asked, "Do you really believe that the Bible is true?" I quickly responded with an abrupt Yes! and then immediately asked him a question about math to change the subject. I didn't know what to say! I had the compassion, and I felt compelled to express it, but I didn't know how.

Much later I came in contact with a group that said, "If you can read, you can share your faith." I could read, so that was good news to me! One of the members of the group took me out to a local university campus so I could learn how to share my faith in Jesus Christ. There we were in a large cafeteria at lunch time with hundreds of students scattered throughout the room eating and studying. I insisted on doing it alone, so I began searching for a guy sitting by himself. There he was, reading the school paper. I asked, "Would you mind answering a few questions on a religious survey?" He didn't seem to mind, in fact, he seemed eager to cooperate. After the survey, I asked if I could share a little booklet with him that really makes sense. Again, his response was very positive.

When I finished reading the booklet, which explained how a person could come into a personal relationship with God, I asked, "You wouldn't want to do that, would you?" Obviously, my expectations of a positive response at this point were not very high. His comeback to me was absolutely terrifying. He said, "Yes, I really would!" Instantly, I came to his rescue with, "Well, maybe you didn't understand the booklet; let me read it over to you one more time." I had only read it a couple of times myself. He patiently allowed me to re-read the booklet.

When I finished, I asked, "Now, you probably wouldn't want to do that, would you?" He said: "Yes, I've been thinking about this whole issue of God and purpose in life for weeks, and I'd like to enter into a relationship with God through Jesus Christ. I'd like to pray that prayer right now!" I nervously said, "Here?" He replied, "Where else?" I didn't even know where I was, and I certainly didn't know where else we could go. I was stuck. So there in the cafeteria before God and everybody, this young man prayed to receive Jesus Christ as his payment for sin. I couldn't believe it. I had never seen anything like this before, and right there in the cafeteria! I was so excited that I immediately moved on to another table to talk with another student. The identical experience occurred. This was too much. Two for Two!

With that experience I was "bumpin' heaven" and began to share that little booklet everywhere I went to everything that breathed. *Then I caught myself!* I caught myself sharing my personal faith in Jesus Christ only because I had a good method, not because I had compassion at all. Methods are good and necessary, but they are absolutely useless without the compassion to energize them.

"Happy is the person who demonstrates compassion." Remembering your own personal experience with the mercy (compassion) of God in time of need should give you a greater motivation and heightened sensitivity to the needs of those around you. Demonstrating compassion is extending relief to others under the excruciating pains of life. It's serving as a helping and healing agent in the relationships of life. Are you showing compassion, or are you so caught up in your methods and activities that your compassion is crowded out?

Pure in Heart

"Blessed are the pure in heart, for they shall see God."

At first glance "pure in heart" seems as if it belongs in the vertical focus, but a study of this phrase throughout both Old and New Testaments will show that it refers to the horizontal relationships of a believer. In Peter's first letter he encourages the believers to "fervently love one another from a pure heart" (I Peter 1:22).

Peacemakers

"Blessed are the peacemakers, for they shall be called sons of God."

The "peacemakers" are not those who carry the signs "Make love—not war!" Peacemakers are those who make peace where there is no peace. Jesus was the greatest peacemaker, for He made peace between the holy God and sinful man where there was nothing but enmity and division.

The believer is to make peace where there is no peace. When dissension builds in your business relationships, be a peacemaker! When the antagonistic cliques form in your neighborhood, be a peacemaker! When your marriage is torn by tension, be a peacemaker! In most situations when you don't pursue the peacemaker stance in relationships, you *make a maximum contribution* to the spread of warfare.

Rejoice in Persecution

"Blessed are those who have been persecuted for the sake of righteousness, for theirs is the kingdom of heaven. Blessed are you when men revile you, and persecute you, and say all kinds of evil against you falsely, on account of Me. Rejoice, and be glad, for your reward in heaven is great, for so they persecuted the prophets who were before you."

Notice the reason for the persecution Jesus speaks of. It's not for attacking someone or for lack of tact, but "for the sake of righteousness." Those who have been hungering and thirsting for righteousness will be noticed by the world. That consistent walk with God's standard makes people uncomfortable, just as the righteousness of Christ made many of those around Him uneasy. There is reason to "rejoice, and be glad" when somebody notices.

While I was a campus minister in the Southwest I witnessed some persecution, but for the wrong reason. Five young men in green blazers descended on the campus student center. They carried stacks of little black Bibles under their arms and used them in a very offensive manner. I watched them operate. One of the "green coats" walked up to a student in the hallway, stuck a Bible in the student's stomach, and said, "Are you saved?" The student's natural reaction was, "From what?" After about forty-five minutes of aggression, the "green coats" were thrown out of the student center by the director. As the martyrs sauntered out exhibiting saintly smiles, they said, "Praise the Lord, we've been persecuted for His name's sake." Unfortunately, it was more for their own name's sake, for their insensitive and odious approach. That was persecution for the wrong reason.

The proper reaction when we are persecuted for righteousness' sake is to "rejoice, and be glad." "Rejoice" I can handle; it's the "be glad" that bothers me. "Be glad" is the word in Greek from which we get "celebrate." Rejoice and celebrate when you are persecuted for righteousness.

A few years ago we had the privilege of ministering on a university campus where there was a seventy percent Jewish population. One day I was on the sixth floor of the men's dormitory talking with a student who called himself "the rabbi of the sixth floor." As we talked, another student stepped off the elevator, positioned himself at my right side, and proceeded to stare two holes right through me. I turned to him and said, "Hi!" He didn't move a muscle or utter a sound. I thought, "He just isn't ready to talk yet. Some people need to warm up a little." So I continued talking with my "rabbi" friend. It was evident that my silent friend wanted my attention, so I turned to him again. "Did I do something to offend you?" To my surprise he broke his silence with, "There are some of us who are willing to die to stop your activity on this campus." That was, without a doubt, the most startling message I had ever received. I mumbled around a little in a state of paralysis. He repeated himself all over again. (He really didn't have to say it again. I heard him the first time!) He was a member of the J.D.L. (the Jewish Defense League— known for bruising bodies, bombing buildings, and the greatest enemy of Israel today), and with their background in mind, I believed every word he spoke!

Rejoice, and be glad in this kind of persecution? Let's say that after my jolting confrontation I called up my staff team and friends and invited them to a party the following Saturday night. They would probably ask, "What's the party all about—somebody's birthday?" "No, we may all be dead by Sunday morning!" Rejoice and celebrate! That's mighty strange! You don't throw parties and celebrate in light of the fact of your imminent destruction! However, this isn't the only frame in Jesus' portrait of a happy believer that is somewhat strange. They're all strange, because His focus differs so greatly from that of the average believer. A happy believer moves to a different drumbeat than the rest of the world.

Weird-for-Jesus Movement

I certainly don't mean to imply that this different drumbeat has anything to do with the "weird-for-Jesus" movement. Jesus is not out to make you weird—just different. (If you're weird, Jesus didn't make you that way. You did it all by yourself!) The different drumbeat comes when we are living life according to very unique principles. We find true happiness through such distinctive principles as being poor in spirit, mourning, and meekness. That's quite a contrast to the selfish pride, the reveling, and the reactionary tendencies which permeate society. There's also a great difference between the merciful, pure in heart, peacemaker lifestyle and that which is non-compassionate, deceitful, and contentious. Truly happy people move to a different drumbeat than the world does.

Horizontal Process

There is an interesting interchange between the vertical and the horizontal relationships. The link between what you are and what you do is critical. The two are inseparable. Let's take a brief look at the innerlocking nature of the Beatitudes.

VERTICAL	HORIZONTAL
Poor in spirit	Merciful
Mourn	Pure in heart
Meek	Peacemaker
Hunger and thirst	Rejoice in persecution

The first four serve as the basis for the last four. Before you can truly be *merciful* (compassionate—a healing agent toward others) you must be *poor in spirit* (anti-pride—a right evaluation of yourself before God). When you have a prideful spirit, it's virtually impossible to demonstrate compassion and lift another person up, because that person could become a threat to you. Before you can truly be *pure in heart* (honest— right motives), you must be one who *mourns* (hating that which keeps you from God). The genuine *peacemaker* (making peace where there is no peace) must be one who is *meek* (no need to react—a quiet controlled strength).

The final couplet centers around righteousness. Those who are *hungering and thirsting for righteousness* (Christ-likeness— walking consistently with God's standard) progressively find true satisfaction in their lives. When this is noticed by the world, every possible attempt is made to discredit the reality of the satisfied, righteous lifestyle. If you are hungering and thirsting for righteousness, you should *rejoice and be glad* when persecuted for it, because someone actually noticed. The righteous lifestyle is a witness in itself to the fact that the personal God of the universe is alive and well.

This interchange between the Beatitudes is not the only place in the New Testament where the horizontal process is evident. After he has discussed the vertical relationship in John 15:1-11, Jesus turns to the horizontal relationships between both believers and non-believers. The relationship with other believers is characterized by "loving." The relationship with non-believers is characterized by "bearing witness." Each of these builds on the vertical relationship of abiding in the Lord.

Another example of this building process is in Romans 12. After the offering of your body (12:1) and the overhauling of your mind (12:2) (the vertical relationship), you are to obtain a servant's heart (12:3), operate within a body of believers (12:4-8), and overflow into the world through love without hypocrisy or vengeance (12:9-21) (the horizontal relationship).

VERTICAL

John 15:1-11— Abide	Romans 12:1—offer your body
	Romans 12:2—overhaul your mind

HORIZONTAL

John 15:12-17— Love	Romans 12:3—obtain a servant's heart
	Romans 12:4-8—operate in a body
John 15:18-27— Witness	Romans 12:9-21—Love and return good for evil

Horizontal Projection—Light

In the same way as the vertical relationship is identified by one word—*salt*—so the horizontal relationship can be condensed into one word—*light*. Immediately following the mention of the *salt* of the earth, Jesus discusses the *light* of the world. He says: "You are the light of the world. A city set on a hill cannot be hidden. Nor do men light a lamp, and put it under the peck-measure, but on the lampstand; and it gives light to all who are in the house" (Matthew 5:14-15).

Jesus makes it clear that every believer is a light. The believer is to dispel the spiritual darkness in the world by allowing his light to shine. It's unthinkable to light a lamp and then cover it up. The natural place for a functioning light is on a lampstand so that the light spreads throughout that particular area of the house. Jesus continues, "Let your light shine before men in such a way that they may see your good works, and glorify your Father who is in heaven" (Matthew 5:16). The horizontal projection is not something you *say*, but something you *do*. Good works are not heard, but seen.

So the vertical and horizontal relationships are brought into focus as we begin to understand the dynamic couplet of *salt and light.* Happy people move to a different drumbeat than the world. They are *salt (in view of the decay in the world)* and they are *light (in view of the darkness in the world.)* Are you a happy person?

Four

A SATISFIED LIFESTYLE!

"Do you think that Adam had a navel?" "How many angels could sit on the head of a needle?" "Who will populate the millenial kingdom?" "Who are the two witnesses of Revelation?" "What is the proper mode of water baptism?" "Does God perform miracles today?" "Is it a sin to drink alcoholic beverages?" With these and countless other extremely "important" questions of life exploding all around me, I felt sick to my stomach. There I sat in my sixth year of Greek and my third year of Hebrew, learning the holy languages without learning to be holy.

I remember the day that the queasy feeling in my stomach reached the intolerable point. I'd had it! The comment that topped it all off was made by a student in the back of the room. He said to another student: "You know, I believe the Lord is pleased with my new method of devotions. I simply work through my Greek vocabulary and grammar cards every morning." I started to chuckle at what I had overheard, but when I turned around to share in what I thought was a joke, I realized that he was actually serious. I could hardly sit through the rest of the class.

Immediately after the class I drove over to a nearby park and sat there with my Bible. The choice was becoming clear to me. Either I could give in to the process of being embalmed by all the intricacies of theological hair-splitting, or I could make it my primary goal to know and experience the true Christian lifestyle. I'd observed many leaders within Christianity who had already spiritually expired and were simply awaiting burial. I could see my own life pointed in the same direction. It amounted to the emasculation of genuine Christianity.

That day in the park I saw who I really was before God as I began meditating on Matthew 5. When I came to "Blessed are those who hunger and thirst for righteousness, for they shall be satisfied," I realized the battle that awaited me. The battle was for true satisfaction on the gut level, satisfaction in the heart and in the mind before the holy God of the universe, satisfaction in my relationships with the Lord, my family, my friends, and my ministry. What a powerful promise! In the battle for true satisfaction my function is to "hunger and thirst for righteousness," to desire it strongly enough to do something about it. This verse was coming alive and burning inside me.

So What?

My former reaction to a "heavy" insight would have been to write it down so I could speak on it some day. This was different. I began to see the utter emptiness in having my intricate theological filing system when my life itself lacked a sanctified filing system. I decided that day that I knew absolutely nothing. I resolved in my heart never to speak on anything without first knowing it experiencially. My byword became "So what?" So what if the Bible is the infallible revelation of God? So what if Jesus was truly the God-Man? So what if Jesus is coming back again? So what difference does it make in my life? That's the proper question. To possess the knowledge that the Bible is the inspired Word of God, that Jesus is truly the God-Man, that Jesus is coming back again without that knowledge affecting a person's lifestyle is the emasculation of Christianity.

From the very beginning of Jesus' ministry He made this emphasis crystal clear in His teachings. In His most significant message recorded in the Bible Jesus addressed Himself to the subject of a righteous lifestyle. His audience consisted of people who had been heavily influenced by the teachings of the Pharisees, and no doubt the prevalent question in their minds with regard to this new religious leader was "How do the teachings of Jesus square with the law of Moses and the teachings and practices of the Pharisees?"

Precepts of Righteousness

Having painted the portrait of righteousness in the Beatitudes, Jesus proceeds to answer this obvious question in the rest of the Sermon on the Mount. Concerning the Mosaic Law He says, "Do not think that I came to abolish the Law or the Prophets; I did not come to abolish, but to fulfill. For I say to you, until heaven and earth pass away, not the smallest letter or stroke shall pass away from the Law, until all is accomplished" (Matthew 5:17-18). He's making it clear that He had no intention of destroying or annulling the law of Moses. On the contrary, the purpose of His coming was to fulfill or accomplish every aspect of the Law. Jesus, the Messiah, would fulfill every prophecy contained in the Old Testament and answer to every letter or partial stroke of a letter in the written Word.

After Jesus has set the stage for His message by indicating where He stood with respect to the Law, He illustrates where He differs with the Pharisaical teaching of the Law. He uses six quotations from the Mosaic Law to expose the error of the Pharisees.

Murder and Adultery

In the first two laws Jesus says that the interpretations of the Pharisees were not comprehensive enough. They didn't go deep enough to the heart of the matter. Behind murder is the sin of anger. "You have heard that the ancients were told, 'You shall not commit murder'; and 'Whoever commits murder shall be liable to the court'; but *I* say to you that every one who is angry with his brother shall be guilty before the court' " (5:21-22). And behind adultery is the sin of lust. "You have heard that it was said, 'You shall not commit adultery'; but *I* say to you, that every one who looks on a woman to lust for her has committed adultery with her already in his heart' " (5:27-28).

Divorce

Then in the third law Jesus shows how the Pharisees could fall into the opposite error—laxity. He says, "And it was said, 'Whoever divorces his wife, let him give her a certificate of dismissal'; but *I* say to you that every one who divorces his wife, except for the cause of unchastity, makes her commit adultery; and whoever marries a divorced woman commits adultery" (5:31-32). Jesus probably introduces the quotation from Deuteronomy 24:1 because it was a passage misused by the Pharisees to justify their lax attitude toward divorce. One scholar paraphrases the words of Jesus as follows: "You have heard of the appeal of Jewish teachers to Deuteronomy 24:1 in the interest of substantiating a policy which permits husbands, freely at their own pleasure, to divorce their wives simply by providing them with a duly attested document of the transaction."[1] So Jesus is speaking not against the Mosaic Law, which permitted divorce in some cases, but against the Pharisees' lax teaching that divorce could be permitted for insignificant reasons.

Oaths

In the fourth law Jesus exposes the Pharisees' deceitful use of oaths. "Again, you have heard that the ancients were told, 'You shall not make false vows, but shall fulfill your vows to the Lord. But I say to you, make no oath at all; either by heaven, for it is the throne of God; or by the earth, for it is the footstool of His feet; or by Jerusalem, for it is the city of the great King" (5:33-35). The interpretations of the Pharisees were interesting. They said, "Whoever swears by the temple, that is nothing; but whoever swears by the gold of the temple, he is obligated." Another tradition said, "Whoever swears by the altar, that is nothing, but whoever swears by the offering upon it, he is obligated." The Pharisees used these subtle twists to deceive people, and those who were not familiar with their traditions were easily tripped up. Jesus clears it up by saying, 'But let your statement be, Yes, yes or No, no; and anything beyond these is of evil" (5:37). When you mean yes, say Yes, and when you mean no, say No!

Retaliation

In His fifth illustration of the contrast between the righteousness of the Pharisees and the precepts of God, Jesus demonstrates further their misunderstanding of the intent of the Law. He says, "You have heard that it was said, 'An eye for an eye, and a tooth for a tooth.' But I say to you, do not resist him who is evil; but whoever slaps you on your right cheek, turn to him the other also" (5:38-39). This particular law was given as a restraint on runaway vengeance. It was not intended as a license for vengeance. The righteous attitude should be a willingness to suffer loss or acquire a bruise, rather than being quick to get back at someone.

Love Your Enemies

The final law used by Jesus to illustrate the Pharisees' misuse and misunderstanding of Scripture was in regard to loving your neighbor. "You have heard that it was said, 'You shall love your neighbor, and hate your enemy.' But I say to you, love your enemies, and pray for those who persecute you" (5:43-44). "And hate your enemy" was added to the Mosaic Law by the Pharisees. Jesus picks up on their false addition and turns it around—love your enemy.

The precepts of righteousness offer a vital twofold lesson in hungering and thirsting for righteousness. (1) *The truly satisfied lifestyle is a natural result of seeking after the true precepts of righteousness which proceed from the Righteous One Himself.* Any precepts that differ or proceed from another source will not result in satisfaction. (2) *The truly satisfied lifestyle is not governed by a legalistic and detailed letter-of-the-law approach, but a liberated spirit-of-the-law which is grounded in the true precepts of righteousness.* Neither the rigidity of the legalist nor the irresponsibility of the libertine will produce satisfaction.

Practices of Righteousness

Concerning the Pharisees Jesus remarked, "For I say to you, that unless your righteousness surpasses that of the scribes and Pharisees, you shall not enter the kingdom of heaven" (Matthew 5:20). Jesus claimed to be in alignment with the Law, yet at this point He says that the Pharisees' teachings and practices were not good enough to qualify a person to enter the Kingdom of God. That must have been a shocking statement to His listeners. How could anyone act more righteously than the extremely religious Pharisees? On the one hand, Jesus put their minds at ease by lifting up the Mosaic Law. On the other hand, He shook them up a little by His comment about the righteousness of the Pharisees. In both ways He stirred up their interest to listen to Him further.

The Pharisees were the strictest religious order in Judaism. In fact, it would be more proper to refer to them as a fraternity. They were known as the "separatists" because they separated themselves from anyone outside their fraternity. They even separated themselves within their fraternity according to their degree of righteousness. The Pharisees were bound by two vows—tithing and purification rites and it was from these two vows that many of their unending traditions arose. Their traditions were supposed to supplement the Mosaic Law, but instead they smothered it.

Profession without Possession

Throughout the Gospels Jesus refers to the Pharisees as hypocrites. There seem to be at least five dimensions of their hypocritical nature. *First, they were professing righteousness but did not actually possess it.* Theirs was a false piety. Their "righteous" traditions made the Word of God of no effect (Mark 7:13). They acted as God's representatives but put aside the commandments of God for the traditions of men (Mark 7:7-8).

Feather-pluckers

Second, the Pharisees were "hyper-critical." They were hair-splitters, nit-pickers, and feather-pluckers. They majored in the minors while completely overlooking the weightier issues. They would be careful to "strain out a gnat" (the smallest) and carelessly "swallow a camel" (the largest). They appeared clean and alive on the outside but were filthy and dead on the inside.

Third, the Pharisees emphasized the letter over the spirit of the Law. They worshipped the letter of the Law meticulously while denying the spirit of it. In order to put every possible ordinance into a nice, neat package, they gave extensive opinions concerning the application of the Law. These steps of application replaced the effect and importance of the Law itself.

Fourth, the Pharisees were great at making absolutes out of non-absolutes. This dimension is simply a facet of the previous one. In their attempt to tie every detail or letter of the Law down, they made their explanations and applications of the laws just as absolute as the Law of God. A good example of this practice was the way they handled the oaths. They made the absolute spirit of an oath (your yes should be yes and your no, no) ineffective by setting up new oaths as absolute. (If you swear by the temple, that is nothing. But if you swear by the gold of the temple, that is binding). (See Appendix 2, "The Hairy World of the Non-absolutes.")

Showmanship

Fifth, the Pharisees drew the condemnation of men on the acts of righteousness before God. In doing their righteous acts, which should have been rendered only to God, they went out of their way to display them publicly. Obviously, in addition to the praise they sought, they also solicited a great deal of negative reaction. The most common example of this was the practice of praying in the most conspicuous place possible. This practice distinguished the Pharisees in a crowd, but who needs that kind of distinction? Some would respond, "How religious!" but most would say, "How disgusting!" It was also disgusting to God, for the act of righteousness (prayer) is to be a private expression of devotion to Him. It is not intended for public consumption.

Unfortunately, each of these dimensions of Pharisaism is still alive in all of its ugliness within Christianity today. According to Jesus they can have no part in the satisfied lifestyle He came to offer mankind. Maybe that's the reason why so many believers are suffering in a state of non-satisfaction. (Some even glory in it—the less satisfaction the better!) Let's take a look at how these dimensions of hypocrisy are illustrated further in this dynamic message of Jesus.

In the next section of the Sermon on the Mount Jesus focuses on the righteous practices of the Pharisees. His words here are most convicting when they are applied to the twentieth century Christian lifestyle. He begins with, "Beware of practicing your righteousness before men to be noticed by them; otherwise you have no reward with your Father who is in heaven" (6:1). These righteous acts are very different from the good works mentioned earlier, which are to be seen by others (5:16). The good works Jesus encourages are performed horizontally toward other people, and they serve as the light of God's glory shining in the world of darkness. The acts of righteousness seem to be just the opposite. These are actions performed vertically toward the Lord. The Pharisees were drawing the attention of others upon these private vertical actions. This brought condemnation from the world and nullified the actions before the Lord.

Don't Sound the Trumpets—Give Secretly

Jesus discusses three acts of righteousness—giving, praying and fasting. The first act of righteousness is giving: "When therefore you give alms, do not sound a trumpet before you, as the hypocrites do in the synagogues and in the streets, that they may be honored by men. Truly I say to you, they have their reward in full. But when you give alms, do not let your left hand know what your right hand is doing; that your alms may be in secret; and your Father who sees in secret will repay you" (6:2-4).

There were thirteen trumpet-shaped treasury boxes located in the temple of Jerusalem where people could deposit their gifts. We may understand the Pharisees' practice by using our money exchange as an example. A person would deposit 100 pennies instead of a dollar bill and thus "sound the trumpet." Naturally, this would arouse the attention of the people in the area and imply to them that "Brother Joseph" gave a lot of money. Giving is an act of righteousness to be exercised privately before the Lord. When it's made public so that others will notice, the applause and the recognition received by the giver is his only reward.

Pray Secretly

The second act of righteousness is praying. Again Jesus states what the practice should not be: "And when you pray, you are not to be as the hypocrites; for they love to stand and pray in the synagogues and on the street corners, in order to be seen by men. Truly I say to you, they have their reward in full. . . . And when you are praying, do not use meaningless repetition, as the Gentiles do, for they suppose that they will be heard for their many words. Therefore do not be like them; for your Father knows what you need, before you ask Him" (6:5, 7, 8).

Alfred Edersheim, the great Jewish historian, paints an interesting picture of the Pharisee and his praying practices. "Walking behind him, the chances were, he would soon halt to say his prescribed prayers. If the fixed time for them had come, he would stop short in the middle of the road, perhaps say one section of them, move on, again say another part, and so on, till, whatever else might be doubted, there could be no question of the conspicuousness of his devotions in market-place or corners of streets. . . . Nor was it merely the prescribed daily seasons of prayer which so claimed his devotions. On entering a village, and again on leaving it, he must say one or two benedictions; the same in passing through a fortress, in encountering any danger, in meeting with anything new, strange, beautiful or unexpected. And the longer he prayed the better. . . . At the same time, as each prayer expressed and closed with a benediction of the Divine Name, there would be special religious merit attached to mere number, and a hundred 'benedictions' said in one day was a kind of measure of great piety."[2] The attention and admiration received from the public was their full reward. The Lord does not favor such antics and therefore does not reward them.

Next Jesus turns to what is a valid practice of righteousness in praying. He says, "But you, when you pray, go into your inner room, and when you have shut your door, pray to your Father who is in secret, and your Father who sees in secret will repay you" (6:6). The real test of true righteousness in praying is what you do when you are alone. He suggests that we pray in secret in a private room. The most important aspect of Christ's words is not *where* to pray, but *how* to pray—privately!

Jesus offers a short (approximately 30 seconds) model prayer. "Pray, then, in this way: 'Our Father, who art in heaven, hallowed be Thy name. Thy kingdom come. Thy will be done, on earth as it is in heaven. Give us this day our daily bread. And forgive us our debts, as we also have forgiven our debtors. And do not lead us into temptation, but deliver us from evil. For thine is the kingdom, and the power, and the glory, forever. Amen' " (6:9-13). What a contrast to the practices of the Pharisees!

Fast Secretly

The third act of righteousness is fasting. "And whenever you fast, do not put on a gloomy face as the hypocrites do; for they neglect their appearance in order to be seen fasting by men. Truly I say to you, they have their reward in full. But you, when you fast, anoint your head, and wash your face; so that you may not be seen fasting by men, but by your Father who is in secret; and your Father who sees in secret will repay you" (6:16-18). Fasting is the controlling of the will in the abstinence of food for a period of time for the purpose of personal devotion to God. Again, because of the private and vertical nature of fasting, it is not meant to have an audience.

These practices of righteousness are filled with significant insights to guide our hungering and thirsting for righteousness. The principle of private focus is predominant—*the truly satisfied lifestyle practices acts of righteousness only before God!* Giving, praying, and fasting are not the only acts of righteousness, but are specific examples which are representative of all such actions of man toward God. For example, praise and thanksgiving are certainly represented in the act of prayer; meditating on the Word of God in the act of fasting.

Each act of righteousness should be evaluated as to *motive*. Are you looking for praise and/or acceptance from others through the performance of this act? How many times have you prayed to the Lord and consciously altered your prayers according to those who were listening? I can't count the times in my own life. How detestable that must be to the Lord! Think of it! You are talking to the God of all creation while searching for the words that will bring praise or acceptance from other creatures. Why do you say, "Thank the Lord," or, "Praise the Lord," in your conversation with other believers? Why do you pray at the restaurant before each meal? For praise, for acceptance, because you think that's the spiritual thing to do? We must evaluate the motives that linger behind all our actions—especially in our acts of righteousness toward the Lord.

Each act of righteousness should also be evaluated as to its value as *testimony*. Does the act draw the contempt of non-believers on acts of righteousness toward God? Even if your motive is correct, you may still be drawing the contempt of others. Maybe your restaurant prayers need to be more private. Any public display before the world of the acts of righteousness are questionable, to say the least; prayer and praise demonstrations, vast giving campaigns. We seem to fall into the trap of making public spectacles of our acts of righteousness. These massive spectacles make for outstanding news print, but the Lord is not impressed. He jealously desires our personal devotion to Him to be absolutely personal—shared with no one. Even in public worship services where we validly lift up our voices in praise, offer our thanks, give our money, or fervently pray together, *we must be careful not to violate the principle of private focus on the Lord. To violate this principle cheapens our vertical relationship, draws the contempt of non-believers, nullifies the effect of the act, itself, and drains the Christian lifestyle of true satisfaction.*

Priority of Righteousness

The portrait, precepts, and practices of righteousness lay the foundation for the satisfied lifestyle. The rest of the Sermon on the Mount builds on this foundation with Jesus' comments concerning the priority, perspective, and false prophets of righteousness. He concludes His message by offering Himself as the Person of Righteousness to be heard and followed in order to experience the truly satisfied life.

To demonstrate the priority of righteousness Jesus contrasts two kinds of treasures—earthly and heavenly. "Do not lay up for yourselves treasures upon earth, where moth and rust destroy, and where thieves break in and steal; but lay up for yourselves treasures in heaven, where neither moth nor rust destroys, and where thieves do not break in or steal; for where your treasure is, there will your heart be also" (6:19-21). The heavenly is permanent; the earthly is temporary. Jesus appeals for single-mindedness in laying up treasures in heaven, because "no one can serve two masters" (6:24).

Yet we can't just go through life laying up heavenly treasures. We do have to live, to eat and clothe ourselves. To this objection Jesus says, "Do not be anxious for your life, as to what you shall eat, or what you shall drink; nor for your body, as to what you shall put on. Is not life more than food, and the body than clothing? *Look at the birds of the air*, that they do not sow, neither do they reap, nor gather into barns; and yet your heavenly Father feeds them. *Are you not worth much more than they*? And which of you by being anxious can add a single hour to his life's span? And why are you anxious about clothing? *Observe how the lilies of the field grow*; they do not toil nor do they spin, yet I say to you that even Solomon in all his glory did not clothe himself like one of these. *But if God so arrays the grass of the field, which is alive today and tomorrow is thrown into the furnace, will He not much more do so for you*, O men of little faith? Do not be anxious, then saying, 'What shall we eat?' or, 'What shall we drink?' or, 'With what shall we clothe ourselves?' . . . *But seek first His kingdom, and His righteousness; and all these things shall be added to you*" (6:25-34).

The truly satisfied lifestyle offers provisions for the necessities of this life and permanence that extends beyond this life as a result of seeking (hungering and thirsting) *His righteousness first.* It's a matter of priorities. Notice that He doesn't say to seek opportunities for service first, but His

Kingdom and His righteousness. It's the satisfied lifestyle that qualifies you for ministry. (See the Appendix—"Priorities Are For People!")

Perspective of Righteousness

In this section (7:1-12) Jesus is careful to comment on the horizontal and vertical perspectives as they relate to the satisfied lifestyle. The theme of the entire section is introduced by the words, "Do not judge lest ye be judged yourselves. For in the way you judge, you will be judged; and by your standard of measure, it shall be measured to you" (7:1-2). He is not saying that believers are never to judge (decide, discern) anything or anyone. He is saying, "Look at yourself first." Don't be like the self-righteous and hypocritical Pharisees. They were quick to judge everyone and everything without looking in their own mirrors.

Judgment

Jesus gives a humorous illustration of this wrong kind of judgment, "And why do you look at the speck in your brother's eye, but do not notice the log that is in your own eye? Or how can you say to your brother, 'Let me take the speck out of your eye,' and behold, the log is in your own eye? You hypocrite, first take the log out of your own eye; and then you will see clearly enough to take the speck out of your brother's eye" (7:3-5). *Don't be quick to judge another believer's actions without carefully examining your own life first.* By following this principle you will be able to see your brother in the proper perspective.

Discernment

Although we are not to be quick to judge fellow believers, we are to be quick to judge matters with respect to non-believers who have blatantly rejected the satisfied lifestyle of righteousness. He says, "Do not give what is holy to dogs, and do not throw your pearls before swine, lest they trample them under their feet, and turn and tear you to pieces" (7:6). To the Jew, the dogs and the swine were considered unclean. He's saying, "Don't share that which is holy and valuable with those who have already rejected it and are violently opposed to it." You must judge that kind of situation and avoid it.

In your judging of believers and non-believers alike you must realize your inadequacy in viewing others without the proper vertical perspective. You must: "Keep on asking, and the gift will be given you; keep on seeking, and you will find; keep on knocking, and the door will open to you. For everyone who keeps on asking, receives; and everyone who keeps on seeking, finds; and to the one who keeps on knocking, the door will open" (7:7-8, Williams translation). *In order to have a proper perspective on righteousness, you must continually seek the Righteous One in prayer.* He sums up the section with, "Therefore, whatever you want others to do for you, do so for them" (7:12). This is the perspective of righteousness necessary for the satisfied lifestyle.

False Prophets of Righteousness

"*Beware of the false prophets*, who come to you in sheep's clothing, but inwardly are ravenous wolves" (7:15). There will be those who pose as teachers and leaders of righteousness, but are not. "You will know them by their fruits. Grapes are not gathered from thornbushes, nor figs from thistles, are they? Even so every good tree bears good fruit; but the rotten tree bears bad fruit. A good tree cannot produce bad fruit, nor can a rotten tree produce good fruit. Every tree that does not bear good fruit is cut down, and thrown into the fire. *So then, you will know them by their fruits*" (7:16-20). Jesus then becomes more specific as to what these false prophets and teachers will say, "Not every one who says to Me, 'Lord, Lord,' will enter the kingdom of heaven; but he who does the will of My Father, who is in heaven. Many will say to Me on that day, 'Lord, Lord, did we not prophecy in Your name, and in Your name cast out demons, and in Your name perform many miracles?' And then I will declare to them, 'I never knew you, depart from Me, you who practice lawlessness' " (7:21-23). There will be many false teachers of righteousness in the world speaking, casting out demons, and performing numerous miracles *in the name of Jesus*. They will even claim Jesus as their Lord. Instead of readily receiving every teacher of righteousness, we must be careful to examine his or her fruit, even those who come in the name of Jesus.

Many counterfeit messages are beaming forth in the name of Jesus today and are being accepted *carte blanche* by followers. Jesus is calling for caution. He says "you will know them by their fruits." Fruit takes time to develop—it's not instantaneous. So we are not to embrace impulsively everyone who comes in the name of Jesus, but to examine cautiously the fruits of each particular teacher. That takes time. *The truly satisfied lifestyle examines the fruit of those teaching in the name of Jesus before tasting of it.*

Person of Righteousness

Jesus sums up His message by offering two options—the narrow gate and the broad gate. The broad gate is wide and leads to destruction and many will enter through it. The narrow gate is small and leads to life, but few will find it! (7:13-34). Jesus expands upon these two options by comparing a wise man and a foolish man. He says: "Therefore, every one who hears these words of Mine, and acts upon them, may be compared to a wise man, who built his house upon the rock; and the rain descended, and the floods came, and the winds blew, and burst against that house; and yet it did not fall; for it had been founded upon the rock. And *every* one who hears these words of Mine, and does not act upon them, will be like a foolish man, who built his house upon the sand.

And the rain descended, and the floods came, and the winds blew, and burst against that house; and it fell" (7:24-27).

Two Alternatives

Here at the close of probably the greatest lecture ever given, Jesus of Nazareth, Master Teacher of the principles for maximum living, offered his audience two alternatives. The first was to hear His true principles of life and act upon them. To follow this alternative was to be like a wise man who built his house upon a rock, and when rains, storms, winds, and floods came, the house stood firm. The other alternative was to hear His true principles and not act upon them. This was to be like a foolish man who built his house upon the sand, and when the same rains, storms, winds, and floods came, his house collapsed. Life in the twentieth century is basically the same as it was in the first. There are still principles for maximum living that are true and very practical, but these principles of life must be acted upon. Otherwise, when the stormy pressures of life come, people will experience breakdowns in their lives in areas like self-esteem, marriage and family, relationships, and purpose for living.

At the end of His great message Jesus answers the question "So what?" Here's so what: *The truly satisfied lifestyle is the result of hearing and acting upon the words of Jesus, the Righteous One.* So what difference does it make? It's the difference between true satisfaction and destructive collapse!

FOOTNOTES

Chapter 4

1. R.V.G. Tasker, *The Gospel According to St. Matthew* ("Tyndale Bible Commentaries") (Grand Rapids, MI: Wm. B. Eerdmans Pub. Co., 1961), p. 66.
2. Alfred Edersheim, *Sketches of Jewish Social Life* (Grand Rapids, MI: Wm. B. Eerdmans Pub. Co., 1974), p. 214.

Five

AN EXPENSIVE LIFESTYLE!

It was early Monday morning, and Mr. Jones was waiting in the service line at the local Volkswagen dealership for a check-up on his "bug." Now, for most people taking your car in for a check-up is relatively simple, but Jones had a way of complicating things. He just couldn't seem to resist the temptation to cross the white line that separated the VW owner from the VW mechanic. Each of the last five times he had brought his "bug" in for service he had stepped across the white line to watch the mechanic. Most mechanics don't like the owners breathing down their necks while they are working (thus the white line), and the mechanic who had worked on Jones' VW the last five times was no exception.

Finally, it was Jones' turn for service. When the mechanic saw who it was he decided immediately that things were going to be different today. It was high time Jones learned to abide by the rules, and he was determined to teach him a lesson. He drove the car across the white line. Jones followed after as usual. The mechanic said, "Jones, let's play a game!" Jones thought for a minute, "O.K., why not?" The mechanic took Jones over to the white line of separation, drew a circle with a piece of chalk, and said, "Jones, I'll bet you can't stay inside this circle while I work on your car." With the confident look of a pool shark about to hustle a novice, Jones said, "You're on, man!" Jones stepped into the circle.

The mechanic then picked up a sledge hammer, walked over to Jones' car, and swiftly delivered a blow to the hood of the little "bug." He looked over at Jones, expecting him to be enraged. Instead he was still standing inside the circle, and he had a smirk on his face. That infuriated the mechanic. He picked up the hammer again and pounded on the car another six or seven times. Jones didn't budge; he was still inside the circle, only now he was laughing so hard that he was holding his side. Jones' reaction caused the mechanic to go berserk. He quickly condensed Jones' car into a true compact. Surely Jones would react now! No, there was Jones still in the circle, lying on the floor howling hysterically.

The exhausted mechanic walked over to Jones, with the sledge hammer still in his hands, and said, "Jones, I've just completely destroyed your VW with this sledge hammer and you just lie there laughing. I don't get it. What's wrong with you?" Jones, still laughing out of control and hardly able to get his words out said, "While you were beating up on my "bug" I stepped out of the circle three times." Jones was playing games while something very serious was going on.

Games Christians Play

The same thing is true of too many believers—they are playing games while something very serious is going on. Silly games. Pointless games. The Who's-Got-More-of-the-Spirit? game. The What-Flavor-Are-You? game. The Come-Forward-and-Join-our-Church game. In most cases these games serve as an effective diversion from the more serious issues of commitment in the Christian lifestyle.

In addition to these games Christians have a flippant way of using the "Let go and let God!" philosophy which aborts authentic commitment to the Lord. Massive appeals are made for an instant commitment of one's life to the ministry, to go to the mission field, or to become a disciple of the Lord—as if it were free! Discipleship is not free. *Salvation is free, but discipleship may cost you everything. It's an expensive lifestyle.*

Requirements of Discipleship

How many millions of people, stirred by the emotional appeal of a preacher, have made a "commitment" to do something or go somewhere for the Lord? How many have actually carried out their commitment? A very minute percentage. Why? Much of the reason comes back to the fact that no one showed the willing, committed person how to count the cost of his/her decision. The requirements of discipleship were not honestly and accurately set forth.

Jesus outlined three primary requirements for discipleship in Luke 14:25-35. There were great multitudes of people following Him around in His ministry, and no doubt many of these people identified themselves to their friends and neighbors as Jesus' "disciples." Jesus didn't turn to them and say, "All who are really with me, stand over here and be counted and register your commitment to me by signing the parchment on that rock." Instead of this bandwagon approach, He forced His audience to think and count the cost of being a disciple by explaining the requirements.

Incomparable Devotion

His first requirement was, and still is, "If anyone comes to Me, and does not hate his own father and mother and wife and children and brothers and sisters, yes, and even his own life, *he cannot be My disciple.*" Jesus, the Author and Teacher of love, is not preaching hate here. Rather He's using the word hate in a comparative sense—compared to your great devotion to Christ, all other relationships should look like "hate." My relationship with Him should be that much superior to any other relationship.

A few years ago I was speaking at a conference of university students. My subject was discipleship. On the first night of the three-day conference, I was impressed with the fact that this group needed to face the cost factor of discipleship. Throughout the second day I worked on my message, "The Bills of Discipleship," based on Luke 14. I had spoken on the passage previously in similar conferences, but it seemed different to me this time. Actually the passage hadn't changed, but I had. Just a few months before our first child had been born to us and I had become a daddy. Tammy was absolutely beautiful! From the moment of birth she was the apple of her father's eye. (As a matter of fact, I took 56 slides in the first 24 hours.) She was my little girl. However, as I read the first requirement for discipleship, my sweet little girl began to cause me a problem.

I had already dealt with my relationships with my "own father and mother and wife," but I had never considered my relationship with Tammy in comparison with my relationship with the Lord. I knew I had to speak on the passage during the conference, but I also knew that I couldn't speak on it without first experiencing it totally. The night before I was to present "The Bills of Discipleship" I wrestled and struggled with the Lord over my little Tammy. I wasn't trying to love her less, but I was struggling over placing my love relationship with her in the proper perspective compared to my love relationship with the Lord. I was afraid to give her over to Him. Intellectually, I knew He could take better care of her than I ever could, but emotionally I was afraid of losing her. After a lot of useless bargaining, fancy dealing, and prejudiced rationalizations, I finally gave up my struggle. (This is the only kind of battle I know of where you can lose and still gain more than if you had won.)

God's revelation doesn't change, but life does. With the inevitable variations in life's circumstances, you must constantly be careful to bring everything into its proper perspective in the light of your vertical relationship. That is the requirement of *incomparable devotion*. He does not say, "You cannot be my *good* disciple," but "you cannot be my disciple" *at all* without satisfying this requirement. Are you willing to put Christ in His pre-eminent place with respect to your closest relationships of life and to your own life?

Unlimited Commitment

The second requirement of discipleship is, "Whoever does not carry his own cross and come after me *cannot be my disciple*" (Luke 14:27). Not only does Jesus require exceptional devotion, He also requires commitment to the point of death. Carrying your own cross implies the kind of commitment that identifies with and follows after Christ's sufferings and ultimate death. In this requirement He is calling for that most conclusive commitment—commitment to the point of death.

The question is not the hypothetical "Are you willing to identify with me to the point of death?" but the very realistic "Are you ready to identify with me to the point of death right now?" Once in a chapel service the speaker asked, "Are you willing to die for the Lord Jesus?" His question elicited a hesitant response from the students, so he posed the question again with more intensity. This time the audience responded with an enthusiastic "Yes!" Then he pulled out a revolver from behind the pulpit. As he pointed the gun toward the people he asked a very different question, "Are you ready to die right now?" Although his demonstration lacked discretion, his point was well made. It's easy to sit in our smugness and make a hypothetical "nod-to-God" commitment, but when we are facing a real crisis, a different kind of commitment is necessary. It's the requirement of *unlimited commitment*.

These first two requirements of counting the cost of discipleship are illustrated by building a tower and going off to battle. Jesus says, "For which one of you, when he wants to build a tower, does not first sit down and calculate the cost, to see if he has enough to complete it? Otherwise, when he has laid a foundation, and is not able to finish, all who observe it begin to ridicule him, saying, 'This man began to build and was not able to finish' " (Luke 14:28-30). The same is true of committing yourself to discipleship. A hasty commitment without deliberation over what it's going to cost may bring ridicule and mockery upon you and your fizzled commitment.

"Or what king, when he sets out to meet another king in battle, will not first sit down and take counsel whether he is strong enough with ten thousand men to encounter the one coming against him with twenty thousand? Or else, while the other is still far away, he sends a delegation and asks terms of peace" (Luke 14:32). In a decision as serious as this, where people's lives are at stake, careful calculation of the cost is a must. Jesus is not attempting to scare anyone away from discipleship, but He is appealing for a realistic examination of what it's going to cost.

Compassionate Mobility

The third requirement reaches the peak of what living commitment can be. In the first He called for greater devotion to Him in comparison to our closest relationships. In the second He called for the commitment to extend to the point of death. Now in the third He calls for everything. "So therefore, no one of you can be My disciple who does not give up all his own possessions" (Luke 14:33). It's one thing to die for a cause, but quite another to live for it. To die for a cause only takes one decision, but to live for a cause involves many decisions, day in and day out.

Christ is not advocating a communistic system for believers, nor is He saying that you must give over all of your possessions to someone or some organization. He does not say *give over*, but *give up!* This is a term meaning to renounce ownership of something. The implication is that you must renounce ownership of your possessions and view them as belonging to the Lord. This renunciation places the disciple in a position where he is free to love others actively, and it's this requirement of *compassionate mobility* that enables him to meet the needs of those around him.

The term "possessions" is all inclusive. It does not refer merely to your material possessions, as many teach. It's much more than that. The possessions Jesus speaks of extend to *your total existence, including your material possessions.* A disciple must not be tied down by anything. You are to renounce ownership of and set apart all that you are and have. Then, you can be a disciple.

Jesus concludes His discussion with a solemn word concerning the usefulness and effect of believers as committed disciples. Again He uses the imagery of salt and the unthinkable possibility of salt becoming ineffective. So it is with discipleship. How unthinkable that a disciple would have any higher devotion than to the Lord, or that he would not give up his total existence including all his possessions! "He who has ears to hear, let him hear" (Luke 14:35).

Results of Discipleship

The requirements of discipleship are stiff and the results of discipleship are overwhelming—both positively and negatively. The writer of the book of Hebrews gives an extensive list of those throughout history who were exceptional in their faith and commitment to the Lord. The list includes men and women who fulfilled the demanding requirements Jesus imposed on would-be disciples. Summing up the results of this daring commitment he says: "And what more shall I say? For time will fail me if I tell of Gideon, Barak, Samson, Jephtah; of David and Samuel and the prophets; *who by faith conquered kingdoms, performed acts of righteousness, obtained promises, shut the mouths of lions, quenched the power of fire, escaped the edge of the sword, from weakness were made strong, became mighty in war, put foreign armies to flight. Women received back their dead by resurrection"* (Hebrews 11:32-35). What a lifestyle! Who could or would pass up that kind of result? Think of it! A discipleship commitment of your life will result in a positive, miraculous lifestyle. Why would anyone need to count the cost of commitment when results like that are promised? That's the kind of abundant life we've all been waiting for.

But wait a minute! There's more. *"Others were tortured, not accepting their release, in order that they might obtain a better resurrection; and others experienced mockings and scourgings, yes, also chains and imprisonment. They were stoned, they were sawn in two, they were tempted, they were put to death with the sword; they went about in sheepskins, in goatskins; being destitute, afflicted, ill-treated (men of whom the world was not worthy), wandering in deserts and mountains and caves and holes in the ground"* (Hebrews 11:35-38). What happened? This is certainly not "the abundant life" we hear about from nearly every "flavor" of Christianity. That's because of the frequent misunderstanding of the abundant life. It is neither the bed-of-roses or the I-win-you-lose lifestyle. On the contrary, the abundant life is filled with trials, sorrows, and losses. Think of Paul's abundant life. He was ship-wrecked, stoned, beaten and left for dead, ridiculed, left alone, imprisoned, etc. I don't know about you, but I could do without that kind of abundance.

The abundant life is actually a *meaningful lifestyle*. It is not without its problems and frustrations, but it views them from the proper perspective. "All things work *together* for good to those who love God" (Romans 8:28). Because God is in control, He can take the bad circumstances of life (He doesn't cause them) and work them together with something else for my good and His glory.

When you realize that the results of discipleship are both negative and positive, you can see that the Christian lifestyle is expensive. The only thing that really matters or that gives true meaning to life is your personal commitment to a relationship with the God of the universe. It's this relationship that provides the unifying thread through all of the particulars of life.

Rationale of Discipleship

The interesting thing about many of the Old Testament

disciples is that they never actually received the promises in which they believed and for which they hoped. They "died in faith, without receiving the promises" (Hebrews 11:13). Yet, their reaction was that they "welcomed them from a distance" (Hebrews 11:13). By faith they mentally apprehended (having seen) and embraced (having welcomed) the promises of God's revelation from a distance. But why? What was it that motivated them to react in this way? What kind of reasoning allowed these people to die in their faith, without receiving the promises? What made them go on in spite of the little they had to show for it? I think the next line explains it: "Having confessed that they were strangers and exiles on the earth" (Hebrews 11:13). That's the pilgrim concept. Those great people of faith realized that they were strangers and exiles on the earth. They had the conviction that their life here on earth was temporary—there was more to come!

The pilgrim concept is described in the next three verses: "For those who say such things make it clear that they are seeking a country of their own. And indeed if they had been thinking of that country from which they went out, they would have had opportunity to return. But as it is, they desire a better country, that is a heavenly one. Therefore God is not ashamed to be called their God; for He has prepared a city for them" (Hebrews 11:14-16). They were not living only for the present—they had a sense of destiny for their future.

In generations previous to ours, believers were more concerned about the "sweet by and by" than the "nasty now and now." The result was the gross neglect of people's needs in the present. With the flood of existentialism came the swing of the pendulum to the other extreme—emphasis on the now. This brought about a much needed awareness of the problems of present life, but in the process the future life has been disregarded.

Neglect of the future life in the Christian's perspective is like giving oneself a haircut without a mirror. Great emphasis should be focused on the believer's future, for his attention to the future affects his present life. This cause-and-effect principle is spelled out most clearly by the New Testament writer

John: "Beloved, now we are children of God, and it has not appeared as yet what we shall be. We know that, if He should appear, we shall be like Him, because we shall see Him just as He is. *And every one who has this hope fixed on Him purifies himself, just as He is pure"* (I John 3:2-3). If our hope is fixed on the future coming of the Lord Jesus, our present life is purified.

Wrangling about the timing of the second coming of Jesus has become one of the most popular pastimes of many Christians. Heated theological discussions rage over whether Christ will come before the tribulation (the pre-tribulation rapture theory), in the middle of the tribulation (the mid-tribulation theory), or at the end of the tribulation (the post-tribulation theory). Who cares? What actual difference does it make in your life whether Christ comes pre, mid, or post tribulation? I have adopted a very firm position. I'm pre-tribulation until the great tribulation begins. At that point I move to a mid-tribulation position for 3 ½ years. Then after the mid-point of the tribulation, I will become post-tribulationist— that position is unshakeable! What really does make a difference is what effect His second coming is having on my life right now!

The balance between the present and the future in the believer's perspective is found throughout the New Testament. Paul, in his second letter to Timothy, speaks of a special reward for those who "have loved His appearing" (II Timothy 4:8). To Titus he writes, "For the grace of God has appeared, bringing salvation to all men, instructing us to . . . *live sensibly, righteously, and godly in the present age, looking for the blessed hope and the appearing of the glory of our great God and Savior, Christ Jesus"* (Titus 2:11-13).

The rationale of the pilgrim concept was the motivating factor that caused the Old Testament believers to go on living a dynamic life of faith in spite of adverse circumstances. Frankly, when I evaluate what keeps me going in the Christian lifestyle in the face of all the trials (that sometimes seem unbearable), the temptations (that are alluring and seem harmless), the conflicts in relationships (that never end), and the general hassles and doubts (that seem to militate against hope itself), I realize that my only hope is the promise of Christ's return. If Christ isn't coming back, then it's all over! If He doesn't come back for us, then the Bible is in error, Jesus is a liar, and we are left without hope. We must live effectively in the present, but our entire perspective becomes faulty when we lose sight of the future. That's the rationale of discipleship—the pilgrim concept.

The Christian lifestyle should not consist of playing games. It's a meaningful, sober and satisfying lifestyle. The requirements are stiff. The results are overwhelming (both negative and positive). The rationale is unearthly. *It's an expensive lifestyle.*

PART TWO

PARTICIPATION—WHO LIVES THE ULTIMATE LIFESTYLE?

Six

TWENTIETH CENTURY MYSTICS AND PHARISEES

A pastor had just moved into a small West Texas cow-town, and he wanted to visit his congregation in the outlying areas. Because of the rough terrain, he went to the local livery stable to purchase a horse and buggy. As he approached the stable he saw a sign that said "Special Sale: Horse and Buggy." He walked in and asked the price of the horse and buggy combo. The owner gave him the incredible discount price of five dollars. The pastor said, "I'll take it!" He quickly handed the man a five dollar bill and jumped up on the buggy. "By the way," the pastor asked, "Why so cheap?" The owner admitted nervously, "Well, you see, this is a religious horse. I mean, he only understands religious language. If you want him to go, you have to say, 'Praise the Lord!' and when you want him to stop, you must say, "Amen!' " The pastor said, "Hey, that's great—I'm a minister." With that he yelled, "Praise the Lord!" and the horse took off.

On the way to his first visit the pastor had to go around several large holes in the ground. (We call them canyons, but Texans call them large holes!) All of a sudden the horse started speeding up as he approached one of the large holes (canyons). The pastor panicked—he forgot the proper signal. He said, "Stop! Whoa! Slow down, boy!" His commands didn't affect the speed or the direction of his horse, which just continued toward the canyon. Finally the pastor remembered the right word, "Amen! Amen!" The horse came to a screeching halt right at the brink of the canyon. The pastor, in a sigh of relief and thankfulness wiped his brow and said, "Whew! Praise the Lord!"

Needless to say that last comment hurled him and his new vehicle into critical condition at the bottom of the canyon. The poor pastor had gotten his signals all mixed up. Many Christians are also at the bottom of some canyon, a spiritual canyon, because they have gotten their signals all mixed up about the source of the Christian life.

Who lives the Christian life—God or man? There seem to be two extreme positions. The first is that God does it all. Man is totally surrendered to God and He lives the Christian life in and through the believer. The second is that man does it all. God saves the believer and then turns him loose to live the Christian life by himself. Both of these are devastating to the dynamic Christian lifestyle.

The God-does-it-all extreme tends toward an eerie, mystical leap for the supernatural. It's the "Let go and let God" approach, with all of its potential for reckless abandon. In most cases it requires a blind leap of faith—you place your faith in faith! "The more faith I can muster the greater the result of experience." It's an extremely subjective lifestyle with too few guidelines. God's performance is the only reality. The believer's responsibility is not taken seriously.

The man-does-it-all extreme tends toward a pious, pharisaical rigidity. It is expressed in a man-made religion filled with traditional and cultural overtones which strangle the very life out of the Christian lifestyle. Very little faith is needed in this extreme—you place your faith *in your performance* of a certain accepted code of conduct. It's an extremely structured lifestyle with an infinitely complex system of do's and don'ts (mostly don'ts). Man's performance in this system is all important. God's power seems irrelevant.

God: Genie or Tyrant?

To one who adopts the God-does-it-all extreme God is

viewed as a powerful, genie-like, God of goodness. He manifests Himself primarily in dramatic, miraculous ways. Naturally this extreme focuses primarily on miracle passages of the Bible. Emphasis is placed on pushing the right buttons and performing the proper formulae to elicit a miraculous type of response from God. In addition to this, because of His kindness and love, God is just waiting to heal every sickness, to make each business deal profit, to save you from all suffering, and to solve your every problem. Life is always to be on top of the pile. God loses a lot of his sovereignty in the view of one who adopts this perspective. He becomes a Genie waiting to respond to the personal whims of the Christian. "Come on, God, over here!" In a sense God ceases to be God.

To the person who follows the man-does-it-all extreme God seems to be a judgmental, tyrant-like God of severity. He's visualized as cold and impersonal, keeping score of our good and bad deeds. Everything is black and white and we must do and not do the right things in order to elicit the grace of God. God is up there with a baseball bat waiting for us to make a wrong move, and when we do, "Whamo!" Life is living underneath piles. God is wrapped up in a nice little package where He can be controlled. When God is seen from this extreme perspective, the control of Him is not through pushing buttons, but through the dimensions of the package itself. He cannot act outside the box, so He is completely predictable. As in the case of the opposite extreme, once again God ceases to be God.

Instant Everythingism

In our modern world with its "now" philosophy, instant reality is all that matters. If it can't be done instantly, then it isn't worth it. This same thinking has permeated the Christian lifestyle. Both the God-does-it-all and the man-does-it-all extremes ignore the process and emphasize instant spirituality.

The *instant experience* of the former extreme and the instant action of the latter extreme refuse to focus on the process necessary for maturity. They view man as totally evil, seeing absolutely no good in him. Because of this evil the God-does-it-all extreme can find no basis for man's potential maturity. Therefore, man must decrease and God must increase. There must be more of Christ and less of man. Although this seems to be right and certainly sounds spiritual, such thinking produces a depersonalization of the believer who has been created in the image of God.

On the other hand, the man-does-it-all extreme finds *no hope* for man's potential maturity because of his evil. Therefore, he reverts to pure performance—only he doesn't perform very well. Even if he did, it would only take one major sin to wipe him out. Again, there does seem to be a kernel of truth here, but those who hold this extreme feel hopelessly beaten down when their performance is poor. *Without a doubt the most dangerous problem in Christianity today is the movement of instant everythingism.*

Spirituality: Perfection?

Right on the heels of instant everythingism is the problem of perfectionism. The God-does-it-all extreme follows a long line of perfectionist-type movements. One example is gnosticism, which arose around the time of Christ and was attacked by Paul in his epistle to the Colossians. Gnostics believed that its true followers could be rescued from this visible, wicked world into a higher world of truth through certain secret knowledge.

The philosophy of gnosticism manifests itself today through movements such as Christian Science and some forms of the meditative arts. Within mainstream Christianity this same thinking has expressed itself over the last 200 years through the perfectionist movement. Early teachers of perfectionism believed that by entering into a relationship with God you become perfect, just as God is perfect. Obviously, this movement didn't last very long. The reason? Somebody in the movement sinned! Then came the movement emphasizing the "second blessing." This is the teaching that you don't become perfect at salvation, but you do become more like God in His perfection with a second blessing experience with Him.

Another group came along and said: "No, it's not the second blessing. It's the baptism of the Holy Spirit (as recorded in Acts) that a person needs to really come alive spiritually." Still others say: "That's not quite right. It's more biblically correct to call this post-conversion experience 'the filling' of the Holy Spirit, and that's what a believer really needs to enter into the higher life." Each of these movements is an attempt to make men perfect or more perfect through some mystical take-over by God.

The man-does-it-all extreme also follows a long line of history. This can be pin-pointed best in the Phariseeism of the first century. Instead of experiencing perfection through a mystical take-over by God, you earn it through your conduct. The resulting problem of legalism was attacked in Paul's letter to the Galatians. The mentality of this extreme leads to a person's becoming entangled with traditions and regulations. People are known for what they do and what they don't do. The pervading attitude is either "I do more than you do!" or "I don't do more than you don't do!" Usually this heavy emphasis on activity moves toward the pharisaical nit-picking of "straining out a gnat and swallowing a camel."

The Uglies

Both extremes are suffering from the uglies. As is commonly true, extreme positions tend to be very similar. The similarities between God-does-it-all and man-does-it-all extremes are numerous. *Both are struggling for perfection by putting sin in a place where it can be man-handled.* The first extreme attempts to blot out the reality of the sin nature through an experience. This must be continually reinforced or the elation is lost to spiritual depression. The second extreme attempts to control the sin nature through intricately defined rules of right and wrong. In order for this to work there must be a constant debate over the "holy list" of do's and don'ts. When faced with the realities of life, this system too fails and spiritual depression sets in.

Neither extreme allows for spiritual depression. When it's present, some deny it and search for another mystical takeover to relieve it; some try to psych themselves out of it; others may resist it as from the Devil. Yet every Christian hurts from spiritual depression at some time in his or her experience. Very few are able to deal forthrightly with the problem, and their perverted ways of handling it produce ugliness.

Another one of the uglies is the pride that develops through both the mystical and the pharisaical extremes. The God-does-it-all extreme causes its adherents to be filled with pride over their experiences. The man-does-it-all extreme fills its followers with pride because of their knowledge. The former enthusiastically live by clichés they've derived from their experiences and from the Word. As one teacher of this position said, "The Bible is just a primer, and nothing more than to thrust us into the supernatural realm of experience with God." The followers of the second extreme rigidly memorize the "right" version of the Bible, and emphasize knowing the Word and living it externally. Both these extreme approaches produce ugly lifestyles, and both breed critical and divisive spirits which lead to even more ugliness.

Of course, it is virtually impossible to identify a person or group within a certain extreme—most swing from one side of the pendulum to the other. Some have the left foot in one extreme and the right one in the other. It's not necessary to draw lines or point fingers of accusation. That only encourages the tyranny of the extremes. We must strive to understand the ideal balance. That's not the easy way, but it must be done. We must answer the question, "Who lives the Christian lifestyle?"

I'm reminded of the famous statement. "The Christian life is not difficult, it's impossible!" In the sense of trying to live the Christian lifestyle without a dynamic relationship with God, the statement is unequivocably true. However, if it is meant to mean more than that, then it's absolutely false. Jesus said, "Enter by the narrow gate; for the gate is wide, and the way is broad that leads to destruction, and many are those who enter by it. *For the gate is small and the way is narrow that leads to life*, and few are those who find it" (Matthew 7:13-14). Jesus says the Christian life is difficult, but you will not find one word in the New Testament that even implies that it's impossible for the Christian in relationship with God. I'd like to change the statement to read: "*The Christian life is not impossible, it's difficult!*"

Seven

SUPERNATURAL CHRISTIANITY

Who does live the Christian life—God or man? A thorough examination of the Bible will demonstrate the answer to this question—both God and man live it. There are certain things that God does and certain things that man does. They both have their parts.

God's Work

With Respect to the Old Nature:

When you were born into this physical world, you became a living being with both material and immaterial characteristics. The material is your body with all of its physical characteristics, and the immaterial is your spirit—your inner being—with all of its spiritual characteristics.

The spiritual characteristics of man include his heart, mind, soul, and character, and it is with man's spirit that God performs His work. It is this aspect of man that can potentially relate to God (God is Spirit), and God's work is to clear away the obstacles so he is able to.

The spiritual characteristics of man are present at this physical birth, but his spirit is dead in that it has no capacity to relate these to God. He can only relate them to the world or to himself (flesh). The spiritually dead man has only his old nature, the one he was born with, and because it is not capable of relating to God, is separate from Him, it is called the sin nature. This is not to say that the old man, who possesses only a sin nature, is not capable of doing good, but these positive moral motions cannot in any way give life to his spirit. Until the spirit is actually reborn, related to God, the will can only exercise itself in relationship to the sin nature, this interlocking relationship being the old man. The old man is the former manner of life before spiritual birth.

Before Spiritual Birth

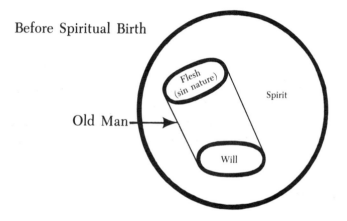

Old Man

At spiritual birth God performs an operation on the old sin nature. If you have entered into that spiritual relationship with God through receiving God's payment for your sin, then you have had this spiritual operation. At the moment of spiritual birth you are united with the death of Christ, so that you actually die with Him. Before spiritual birth you were related only to the flesh (sin nature), but after spiritual birth that relationship is severed and a new one established.

Concerning this Paul says, "knowing this, that our old self was crucified with Him, that our body of sin [flesh] might be done away with that we should no longer be slaves to sin. For he who has died is freed . . ." (Romans 6:6-7). You are legally free from your enslavement to the flesh. Note that the interlocking relationship between the will and the flesh, the old man, was crucified—destroyed! That control relationship is over. While the old man was destroyed, the flesh was not, it was simply "made powerless" over your will. In other words, the will is no longer enslaved to the flesh to do sinful works, although it may still yield to the lusts of the flesh at any time. Through union with Christ's death we have been set free from the control of the flesh—the power of sin.

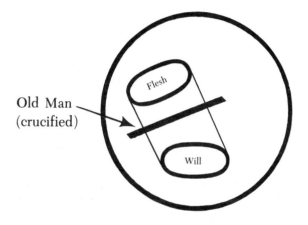

Old Man
(crucified)

With Respect to the New Nature:

Paul continues his explanation by pointing out, "If we have become united with Him in the likeness of His death, certainly we shall be also in the likeness of His resurrection" (Romans 6:5). Through our union with the *death* of Christ we have been set free the control of the flesh, but God didn't leave us dead. Through our union with the *resurrection* of Christ we have been given a new nature that is alive to God. This new nature, our reborn spirit (John 3:6-7), gives us a new capacity whereby we can live in relation to God in our daily experience. The innerlocking relationship between the will and the new nature, our reborn spirit, is called the new man. The new man is our new manner of life in Christ.

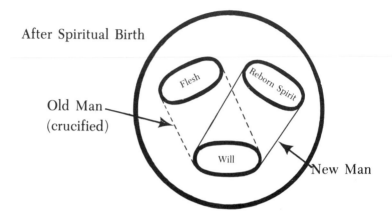

The fact of the new nature (my reborn spirit) means that there is a *good me*. According to Galatians 5:16 we have two options. We can walk by means of the spirit or we can walk by means of the flesh. If "spirit" is taken to be the Holy Spirit instead of my reborn spirit and the flesh is the old sin nature, then there is no *good me*. Either I act through my dirty old sin nature or God, the Holy Spirit acts for me. It doesn't make sense for "spirit" to mean Holy Spirit, but reborn spirit. I am a new creation of God with a new set of desires. I have a new capacity to live for God. Because of God's supernatural operation in my life, there is a *good me!*

So as believers we have a choice—we can walk (exercise our will) by means of the spirit, in our new nature, or walk (exercise our will) by means of the flesh, our sin nature (Galatians 5:16). We have been set free from the control of the flesh through Christ's death and have been given a new capacity to live life toward God through Christ's resurrection. Through this supernatural, spiritual operation of God I can now relate my spirit and its characteristics to God. I'm spiritually alive in Him.

With Respect to the Holy Spirit:

Not only has God set us free to live for Him by giving new life to our spirits, He has come to reside in us permanently through the person of the Holy Spirit. There seem to be two general dimensions of the Holy Spirit's function in the life of the believer—the believer in the Holy Spirit and the Holy Spirit in the believer.

The believer is immersed in the Holy Spirit and the things of the Spirit by what is called the "baptism of the Spirit." The term baptism, is from the Greek word which means "to dip into" something. Figuratively, it means to give a new identification. A white cloth dipped (baptized) into a container of red dye will have a new identification—red. The Holy Spirit's baptism gives a person new identification. Instead of being outside the realm of God, He places us in the body of Christ—we are in Christ.

God views all believers in this eternal position, no matter what their present experience might be. In Christ we are justified—just as if we'd never sinned! "He made Him [Jesus] who knew no sin to be sin on our behalf, that we might become the righteousness of God *in Him*" (II Corinthians 5:21). *In Christ,* "we have redemption, the forgiveness of sins" (Colossians 1:14). "*In Him* you have been made complete" (Colossians 2:10). We have been blessed "with every spiritual blessing in the heavenly places *in Christ*" (Ephesians 1:3). "Therefore if any man is *in Christ,* he is a new creature; the old things passed away; behold, new things have come" (II Corinthians 5:17). Being *in Christ* is a new identification which serves as the foundation for living.

This new identification happens at the time of spiritual birth and this is true of all believers. According to Paul it was true of *all* the Corinthians (I Corinthians 12:12-13), even those who were involved in immorality. It's not for a few superior Christians, but for all believers. Those who believe that the Spirit-baptism is only for a few believers and subsequent to spiritual birth seem to be confusing a certain valid experience they have had with the special enablings of the Holy Spirit illustrated throughout the Bible.

Not only is the believer in the Holy Spirit, but the Holy Spirit is in the believer. The Holy Spirit created the reborn spirit and also resides in it. Yet before delineating what the indwelling Spirit does in the believer, we should note what the Spirit does not do.

What the Spirit Does Not Do!

There are four works of the Holy Spirit that are mistakenly attributed as specific works in the believer today. All of these are talked about by Jesus in the Gospel of John. A thorough examination of the context will show that these popular works of the Spirit are not for believers today. The first one is the convicting work of the Spirit. Jesus tells His disciples that when the Holy Spirit comes, He "will convict the world concerning sin, and righteousness, and judgment; concerning sin, because they do not believe in Me; and concerning righteousness, because I go to the Father, and you no longer behold Me; and concerning judgment, because the ruler of this world has been judged" (John 16:8-11). Notice that He will not convict the believers, but the non-believers. Believers don't need the direct conviction of the Holy Spirit. They have their reborn spirit and the complete revelation of the New Testament that clarifies sin, righteousness, and judgment.

The other three works of the Spirit that are not for believers today were meant specifically for the disciples—guiding, teaching, and bringing to remembrance. With respect to the guiding work of the Spirit, Jesus tells His disciples: "I have many more things to say to you, but you cannot bear them now. But when He, the Spirit of truth, comes, *He will guide you into all the truth*; for He will not speak on His own initiative, but whatever He hears, He will speak; and He will disclose to you what is to come. He will glorify Me; for He shall take of Mine, and shall disclose it to you" (John 16:12-14). The Holy Spirit is to guide the disciples into all *the truth*. *The truth* is a term which normally refers to the written revelation—the Word of God. The New Testament had not yet been written, but Jesus was talking to its future writers. He was telling them that He couldn't relate everything to them at that time, because they couldn't take it, but at the right time the Holy Spirit would guide them into all *the truth*—the Word of God—so that they could write it down. He's referring to the Holy Spirit's work of inspiring the Word of God.

The Spirit's works of teaching and bringing to remembrance also refer to the disciples' involvement in writing the New Testament. Jesus says: "These things I have spoken to you, while abiding with you. But the Helper, the Holy Spirit, whom the Father will send in My name, *He will teach you all things, and bring to your remembrance all that I said to you*" (John 14:25-26). The writers of the New Testament not only wrote divine truth, they also accurately wrote everything (conversations, messages, etc.) that Jesus said to them. The only way they could do such a thing was through the inspiration work of the Holy Spirit. "He will teach you all things and bring to your remembrance all that I said to you" so that the disciples could write these things down in the New Testament revelation. This is not a work of the Spirit for believers today, but was specifically for the disciples and their special task.

What the Spirit Does Do!

Then what does the indwelling Holy Spirit do? There are at least nine facets of God's work in the believer through the Spirit, and although God, the Holy Spirit, can and will do other things, these seem to be His primary functions within the believer (John 14:16,17). (1) *He is the seal of God in us* (Ephesians 4:30). He is like an engagement ring that promises the fulfillment of marriage. The Holy Spirit's presence in our lives is our guarantee that God will continue to do His work in us until the return of Christ.

(2) *He leads us to life*. This work of the Holy Spirit is closely related to His sealing. Paul alludes to this work when he says, "For I am confident of this very thing, that *He who began a good work in you will perfect it* until the day of Christ Jesus" (Philippians 1:6). Through this work of perfecting us God intends to "conform us to the image of His Son" (Romans 8:29). He's leading all believers to Christlikeness—holiness of life. This is not a leading of the Spirit to do this or that. Although believers use that terminology for the workings of the Spirit, the Bible doesn't. There are only two times in the New Testament the believer is said to be led by God—once by the Holy Spirit (Romans 8:14) and once by the reborn spirit (Galatians 5:18). In both cases it is speaking of the universal leading of God into holiness of life. As our seal of God the Holy Spirit is constantly leading us to real life—Christlikeness. In spite of the obstacles or the ups and downs in our moods, He is always moving us toward that goal of being conformed to the image of the Lord Jesus Christ. In this work of leading us to life "the Spirit Himself bears witness with our spirit that we are children of God" (Romans 8:16).

(3)*The Holy Spirit is our enabler* (John 14:16, 26). He is the very source of life and power—the energizer of our reborn spirit which He also created. He is more than just a very powerful force. This is God Himself resident in our lives. He will supply all the resources necessary to live the Christian life. His power is always there and is constant through the reborn spirit, whether we pray for it or not. The supply of power seems to vary according to the need for a specific task or experience. It's like spiritual adrenalin! There are times when His enablement is very clearly recognized for what it is, such as at the time of Pentecost (the coming of the Holy Spirit to indwell believers permanently. This would be a special enablement of the Spirit. When such an obvious work of God is recognized, the natural response is to want more of it.

Many people feel the need to label the experience (the second blessing, the baptism, the filling, slain in the Spirit, etc.), seek it again, propagate it as an experience for everyone, and hold it up as a prerequisite for spiritual maturity.

This kind of experience can become so important ("I can't know God's fulness without it!") that people will do anything to get it. They work themselves up into an emotional state which results in an experience. The experience is labeled as a dynamic work of God and everyone feels great. However, this may not be a work of God, but simply the psychological workings of man. The tragedy of such a chain reaction is that in most cases the original experiences were true sovereign acts of God within the believer. He was especially enabled for a special task, but there is no formula that can reproduce this again. It's a completely sovereign act of God the Holy Spirit for a special circumstance or in a time of great need. God the Holy Spirit works in us "for His good pleasure" (Philippians 2:13). He enables us to do that which is pleasing to God.

(4) *He instills desires in us*. In Galatians 5:16-17 Paul says: "But I say walk by that which is spirit [reborn spirit], and you will not carry out the desire of that which is flesh [old sin nature]. For the flesh sets its desire against that which is spirit, and that which is spirit sets its desire against the flesh" (partial paraphrase). The reborn spirit has spiritual desires in contrast to the desires of the flesh. Before spiritual birth we had only fleshly desires, but from that point on we have spiritual desires through our reborn spirit. These are energized and directed by the Holy Spirit. In his letter to the Philippians, Paul says, "For it is God who is at work in you, both *to will* and to work for His good pleasure" (Philippians 2:13). We are not to dismiss our desires or be afraid of them, but we must be careful to discern between our new desires of the spirit and those of the flesh.

(5) *He intercedes for us*. The Spirit "helps our weakness; for we do not know how to pray as we should, but the Spirit Himself intercedes for us with groanings too deep for words" (Romans 8:26). He is our constant Helper in our finite efforts to relate to the infinite God of the universe.

(6) *He illuminates the Word of God for us*. The nonspiritual man (non-believer) "does not accept the things of the Spirit of God; for they are foolishness to him, and he cannot understand them, because they are [only] spiritually

appraised. But he who is spiritual appraises all things" (I Corinthians 2:14-15). Before spiritual birth we were blinded by the "god of the world" so that we could not see the light of the good news, could not understand spiritual things, and therefore could not accept them. At spiritual birth, the Spirit performed eye surgery so that we "might know the things freely given to us by God" (I Corinthians 2:12). His illuminating work consists of "interpreting spiritual things to spiritual men" (I Corinthians 2:13, paraphrased). Now we can understand and accept the things of the Spirit of God.

(7) *He gives us wisdom.* "But if any of you lacks wisdom, let him ask of God, who gives to all men generously and without reproach, and it will be given to him" (James 1:5). It's a wisdom "not of this age, nor of the rulers of this age" (I Corinthians 2:6). He will give us wisdom so that we can make wise decisions for His glory and our good.

(8) *He works all things together for good.* "And we know that God causes all things to work together for good to those who love God, to those who are called according to His purpose" (Romans 8:28). It's not that He'll work everything out to be good, but that He'll work everything (trials, tragedies, etc.) *together with something else for good.* The tragedy in and of itself is not good, but God will mesh it with something else to produce good.

(9) *He is the giver and worker of gifts.* "Now there are varieties of gifts, but the same Spirit. And there are varieties of ministries, and the same Lord. And there are varieties of effects, but the same God who works all things in all persons. But to each one is given the manifestation of the Spirit for the common good. . . . But one and the same Spirit works all these things, distributing to each one individually just as He wills" (I Corinthians 12:4-7, 11). The variety of gifts are given for the building and equipping of the body of believers, that we might more effectively serve the Lord through our relationships inside and outside the body. The proper exercise of the gifts will cause the growth of the body and will demonstrate a supernatural testimony of God to the world.

Eight

SUPERNATURAL CHRISTIANITY— NATURALLY!

Man's Work

Man's work is always in response to God's work. There are three easy-to-remember words that have been used to describe man's response to what God has done—*know, reckon,* and *yield.* The first two are valid, but the last has been devastating to a balanced understanding of who lives the Christian life. Instead of *know, reckon,* and *yield,* it should be *know, reckon,* and *stop yielding—start yielding*

Know

In Paul's thorough treatise to the Romans he sets forth man's response to God's work. He says: "For if we have become united with Him in the likeness of His death, certainly we shall be also in the likeness of His resurrection, *knowing* this, that our old self [old man] was crucified with Him, that our body of sin [flesh] might be done away with [made powerless], that we should no longer be slaves to sin; for he who has died is freed from sin. Now if we have died with Christ, we believe that we shall also live with Him, *knowing* that Christ, having been raised from the dead, is never to die again; death no longer is master over Him. For the death that He died, He died to sin, once for all; but the life that He lives, He lives to God" (Romans 6:5-10). *We are to know that we are dead to sin through our union with Christ's death, and that we are alive to God through our union with Christ's resurrection.*

Reckon

It is not enough, however, simply to know it. We must also reckon on it. "Even so consider [reckon] yourselves to be dead to sin, but alive to God in Christ Jesus" (Romans 6:11). The word "reckon" doesn't have the same meaning here as it might for a southerner giving an affirmative answer to a question, "Yeah, I reckon!" Reckon means to count on it or act as if it is true. Since it is impossible to see or feel the spiritual operation that God has performed in our bodies, we must count on it as true—believe it! We are commanded to adopt the mental attitude of believing we are freed from sin's power through death and are now alive toward God. We can count on this as true, because it is a fact revealed by God.

In the introduction to his popular book *Psycho-Cybernetics*, Dr. Maltz, a plastic surgeon, tells how he got involved in self-image psychology.[1] The incident that aroused his thinking on this involved a patient—a duchess with a tremendous hump on her nose. She had come to him for plastic surgery, and after the operation displayed a beautiful face with a classic nose. However, though the facts were now different, she continued to think of herself as the ugly duckling. Comparisons of photographs taken before and after were to no avail. Friends and family hardly recognized her and raved over her new beauty. Still, she denied any change had been made. Although she could see that the hump was no longer on her nose, by some strange mental alchemy her nose still looked the same to her. She refused to reckon on the facts revealed in her mirror and consequently she was miserable.

Believers react somewhat as the duchess did. God has

removed us from the power of sin, and yet we look on ourselves as still under its power. By the Holy Spirit, God has created a new capacity in us by which we are alive toward Him, and yet we act as if that capacity does not exist. We look in the mirror of God's Word and see ourselves dead to sin and alive to God, yet we continue to live as though nothing ever happened to us as a result of Christ's death and resurrection. We are to reckon or count it as true. This is not just a superficial belief in something—it means to be *convinced*. When someone is convinced of a matter, he acts on it! In effect, reckoning is an act of the will appropriating God's power to live the Christian life.

Stop Yielding—Start Yielding

The most common teaching at this point is that our proper action is to yield—totally surrender. The notion is that we first know, then reckon, then "let go and let God!" That is not what the passage says, *"Therefore [since God has made you dead to the power of the old nature and made you alive to God through the new nature], do not let sin [the sin nature— the flesh] reign in your mortal body* that you should obey its lusts, and *do not go on presenting the members of your body to sin* as instruments of unrighteousness; but *present yourselves to God as those alive from the dead*, and your members as instruments of righteousness to God" (Romans 6:12-13).

God's work is incredible! He frees us from the bondage of the old sin nature, makes us alive to live for Him through the new nature (reborn spirit), places us in the Holy Spirit with a new identity, and indwells us by the Holy Spirit, through whom we have available to us the same power that spoke the creation of the world into existence. That's supernatural Christianity!

There are two decisive steps after knowing and reckoning. The first Paul expresses in two imperatives, "Do not let sin reign" and "Do not go on presenting." These refer to our sin nature, the flesh. Since we are dead to the flesh, we should stop letting sin reign. "And do not go on presenting the members of your body to sin" explains specifically how someone "lets sin reign," by yielding his will to the flesh and obeying its desires. Paul simply tells us to *stop yielding to the flesh*.

The second action step is "Present yourselves to God." Because we have become alive spiritually it is now possible to make such a presentation to God. We are no longer spiritually dead toward God, but alive in our reborn spirit, our new nature. Paul says we must *start yielding to God* through our reborn spirit. Our supernatural capacity is summed up in the fact that we have a new nature with the resident ministries of God, the Holy Spirit, living inside. Knowing and reckoning on what God has done in freeing us from the power of sin enables us to live for Him, and we must act accordingly—*stop yielding to the flesh and start yielding to the reborn spirit where the Holy Spirit resides. It's "putting off" the old nature and "putting on" the new. It's saying No! to the flesh, Yes! to the spirit.* The believer *grieves the Holy Spirit* by saying Yes! when he should have said No! (Ephesians 4:30), and he *quenches the Holy Spirit* by saying No! when he should have said Yes! (I Thessalonians 5:19).

A very depressed woman came in for counseling a few years ago. She said, "I've got this problem of exaggeration over the phone. I've taken it to the Lord and asked Him to take it away, but He hasn't done a thing." She was aware of what God had done for her problem, but she was then expecting Him to do something He never said He would do. I told her I had a foolproof method of solving her problem of exaggerating. "The next time you exaggerate (or lie) over the phone, stop yourself right there, tell the person you were stretching the truth, and tell them the real truth." She said, "But if I did that, I'd . . . ." I interrupted, "You'd never lie to that person again." With a nod of agreement she said, "Right!"

It's put off, put on! Stop and start! After you know and reckon upon God's work, stop yielding and start yielding. I once heard a counselor ask; "When is a liar not a liar? It's not when he quits lying, but when he stops lying and starts telling the truth. When is a thief not a thief? It's not when he quits

stealing (he may be between jobs!), but when he stops stealing and starts working and giving" (Ephesians 4:25-32).[2]

To sum up, man's work is to know and reckon upon the
spiritual operation of the Holy Spirit, and then to act upon
it—stop yielding to the flesh and start yielding to the spirit.
With this in mind the daily decisions of life can be made with
confidence. Based upon the spiritual operation and the
ministry of the Spirit, the absolute precepts and the guiding
principles of the Word of God, and a confidence in the
indwelling wisdom of God, we can evaluate our circumstances, the counsel of others, our desires and our convictions
in order to live a life pleasing to Him and fulfilling to us.

God's Work Demands Man's Response!

The true balance of who lives the Christian life is 100%
God and 100% man. Now don't panic over that. God's 100% is
much more than man's 100%. Man's part is walking by faith.
"Walking" is what we do, and "by faith" refers to what we expect God to do. The great missionary, William Carey,
expressed the balance when he made his famous statement
"*Attempt* great things for God, and *expect* great things from
God." We do the possible by faith that God will do the impossible. You have all of the enablement necessary to live the
Christian life—so act as if you do. God's work demands man's
response.

The last time our family moved a wonderful thing
happened to us financially. In the sale of our house in Dallas
and the purchase of our house in Newport Beach a lot of
money changed hands. Unfortunately, I'm not used to handling large figures like that in my checkbook. (This is not
because I don't believe in it, but I've always had a cash flow
problem—it's always flowing outward!) When we had been
settled in Newport for only a short time, I realized that the
bank balance was $1,000 more than my checkbook balance. I
couldn't believe it. I called the bank immediately to tell them

that they must have made a mistake. In our financial condition, I just don't lose $1,000. After talking to a bookkeeper and a vice president of the bank, I quickly looked through my checkbook one more time. Sure enough, it came out just the same. I was ecstatic, in shock.

I called my wife to announce our newly discovered wealth. We decided to give the bank a few days (in case they might find a mistake) before we celebrated. Then we went out to dinner. The price of the dinner was almost as much as I thought we had in the bank before the additional $1,000. Believe me, when I wrote that check, it was by faith in what the banker had said. The same is true in the Christian life. We have been told through God's Word what He has done in us and for us, and on that basis we are to write the check—act like it!

Illustrations from the Old Testament

The principle that God's work demands man's response is found throughout the Bible. In the Old Testament biographical illustrations abound. Many of these are briefly listed in the faith chapter (Hebrews 11) of the New Testament. One example of the principle is Noah's life. By faith Noah built a boat. He built it (man's work) in response to God's revelation to Him (God's work). Noah did not "let go and let God." He built the boat! He got his hands blistered and splintered. Noah didn't conjure up the idea, "I think I'll build a boat." He built it in response to God.

The Example of the Life of Christ

The events surrounding Lazarus' death and resurrection offer an excellent illustration of the proper balance. After Lazarus had died, Jesus went to his house and asked, "Where have you laid him?" Jesus knew where they had laid him. He had made the cave where they had laid him. Still, He asked them to show Him. When they arrived before the cave, Jesus said, "Roll away the stone!" Jesus could have rolled away the stone. He could have said, "Stone, roll away!" but He had them do it. But after they had rolled it away, did Jesus walk into the tomb and say, "Now, tell him to get up!" No! *He* told Lazarus to get up and Lazarus got up. Why the change in operation? Dead people don't get up when people tell them to. Dead people only get up when God tells them to. After Lazarus got up, Jesus said, "Take off his grave clothes!" Certainly anyone who could make a person come back to life after "Behold, how he stinketh," could dissolve the grave clothes in the process. Yet He didn't do it; He had them do it. Throughout this experience Jesus was instructing the friends and family of Lazarus to do the possible (locating the grave, rolling away the stone, taking off the grave clothes) by faith that God would do the impossible (raise Lazarus from the dead). That's an example of the balance of who lives the Christian life.

The Teaching of the New Testament

Throughout the various epistles in the New Testament the same balance is clear—*God's work demands man's response*. James says that God "brought us forth by the word of truth, so that we might be as it were the first fruits among His creatures" (James 1:18). That's God's work. He then warns his readers not just passively to enjoy this work of God in them, "but prove to be doers of the word, and not merely hearers who delude themselves" (1:22). That's man's response to God's work.

John puts the balance this way: "And by this we know that we have come to know Him, if we keep His commandments. The one who says, 'I have come to know Him,' and does not keep His commandments is a liar, and the truth is not in him; but *whoever keeps His word [man's work]*, in him *the love of God has truly been perfected [God's work]*" (I John 2:3-6).

In Peter's second letter he first presents God's work: "Seeing that His divine power has granted to us everything pertaining to life and godliness, through the true knowledge of Him who called us by His own glory and excellence" (II Peter 1:3). Then he describes what man's response should be: "Now for this very reason also, *applying all diligence*, in your faith *supply* moral excellence, . . . knowledge, self control, . . . perseverance, . . . godliness, . . . brotherly kindness, . . . love. For if these qualities are yours and are increasing, they render you *neither useless nor unfruitful* in the true knowledge of our Lord Jesus Christ. . . . Therefore, brethren, *be all the more diligent to make certain* about His calling and choosing you; for as long as you *practice these things*, you will never stumble" (II Peter 1:5-8, 10).

Paul's thirteen epistles offer the most thorough treatment of this balance. One of the most popular expressions of the balance from Paul's perspective is also the most often misquoted. In Galatians 2:20 Paul says, "I have been crucified with Christ; and it is no longer I who live, but Christ lives in me." Many people stop right here, so it sounds as if the Christian life is lived totally by God. We must read on. "And *the life which I now live in the flesh I live by faith* in the Son of God, who loved me, and delivered Himself up for me." There's the balance! Now that I have died with Christ and am alive in Christ (because He lives in me), I live my life in this body by faith in Him.

Another popular passage is Philippians 2:12-13. Without an understanding of the proper balance these verses might be very confusing. Paul says, "So then, my beloved, just as you have always obeyed, not as in my presence only, but now much more in my absence, work out your salvation with fear and trembling." You work out your own salvation by living out your Christian faith in obedience to Him. If this verse were all we had, it would seem that man has to live the Christian life all by himself with fear and trembling. But Paul goes on, "For *it is God who is at work in you, both to will and to work* for His good pleasure." There he gives the basis for

man's living the Christian life—"for God is at work in you."
It's 100% God—100% man!

In the book of Romans, a complete treatise by Paul on the
balance of the Christian life, he makes it very clear that God's
work demands man's response. In the first three chapters he
presents man as being in a heap of trouble—guilty before God
because of his sin. In chapters 4 and 5, he explains that
through faith in God's revelation (Jesus Christ) man can be
justified—just as if he had never sinned. The believer is given
a new past! In chapter 6 the believer is described as having a
new position. He's in Christ—dead to sin and alive to God.
Chapter 7 presents the struggle of the believer as he is torn between the sin nature and the new nature, and then in chapter
8 the believer is given a new power—the Holy Spirit. The
resident power of the Holy Spirit, bearing witness with my
spirit that I am truly a child of God, enables me to live out the
Christian life through my new nature (reborn spirit). All of
this is God's work.

Then in chapter 12 Paul turns the corner and sets forth
man's response to God's work. He says, "I urge you therefore,
brethren, by the mercies of God [by what God has done for
you], to present your bodies a living and holy sacrifice, acceptable to God which is your spiritual service of worship. And do
not be conformed to this world, but be transformed by the
renewing of your mind, that you may prove what the will of
God is, that which is good and acceptable and perfect" (12:1-
2). *God's work demands man's response.*

Another complete treatise by Paul on the balance of the
Christian life is the book of Ephesians. In the first three
chapters the believer is not told even one thing that he must
do. Rather he is told what God's work is in his life. He has
blessed us with every spiritual blessing. He has already seated
us in the heavenly places. We have the same power that raised
Jesus from the dead. Paul is trying to overwhelm us with what
has been done in our lives by God. Then in the last three
chapters Paul gives us 33 or 35 things to do. The whole theme
of the book is, "Look what God has done for you! Now will
you act like it?" It's 100% God—100% man.

The letters to the Galatians and the Colossians are reworkings of Romans and Ephesians respectively in an attempt to bring the balance of the Christian life to bear upon extreme situations. Galatians deals with the problem of the man-does-it-all extreme, with its intricate code of conduct. The message is that we are free in Christ from the burden of the Law, because we have been made spiritually alive through the reborn spirit. "It was for freedom that Christ set us free; therefore keep standing firm and do not be subject again to a yoke of slavery" (Galatians 5:1). Colossians deals with the problem of the God-does-it-all extreme, with its demand for the fulness of God.

There is a heavy emphasis on the Holy Spirit in this extreme (heavier than Jesus said should be) in experiencing the fulness of God. There is no doubt that the Holy Spirit's work is indispensable in our experience of the fulness of God. However, in Paul's book on fulness and how to experience it (Colossians), he never mentions the Holy Spirit once! Paul says that in Jesus Christ "all the fulness of deity dwells in bodily form, and in Him you have been made complete and He is the head over all rule and authority . . . [You have] been buried with Him in baptism, in which you were also raised up with Him through faith in the working of God, who raised Him from the dead. And when you were dead in your transgressions and the uncircumcision of your flesh, He made you alive together with Him, having forgiven us all our transgressions" (Colossians 2:9-10, 12-13).

Since you have the fulness of God dwelling in you, don't let anyone rob you of your appropriation of this fulness by emphasizing religious activities or unusual experiences. Paul's advice for experiencing fulness is to "hold fast to the Head" (Christ), because "Christ is all and in all." He doesn't say to seek some dynamic experience with the Spirit or to hold fast to the Spirit, but rather to hold fast to the Lord Jesus. As we do that, we are cooperating with the Holy Spirit's work in us.

One Hundred Percent

The principle that God's work demands man's response gets right down to everyday life. I can't count the times that I've heard a person give his/her testimony in a balanced way, and then when confronted with the question of who accomplished it, they move to the God-does-it-all extreme. After a testimony is given, I'll usually say, "You certainly did a good job!" In nearly every case the response will be, "Oh, I didn't do it. God did!" Somehow I was absolutely sure I saw his mouth move up there. Such a response is innocent in that the person is anxious not to take the credit, but the truth is that he or she spoke, even though it was God who enabled him or her to do so.

When I speak before an audience, I use every communicative principle necessary and do the best I can. I work hard, doing it by faith that God has done His work and is doing His work in me to enable me to speak. My work is temporary (keep the audience awake for 45 minutes and present the truth to them in an understandable way), while at the same time I'm counting on God to be working a permanent work in their lives. I speak by faith. It's 100% God—100% man. *God's work demands man's response, but man's response is absolutely worthless without God's work.*

In our desire for the Ultimate Lifestyle we tend to downplay that which is truly supernatural (God's spiritual operation and the present ministry of the Holy Spirit) and elevate to supernatural status experiences which may be nothing more than inner psychological rumblings. We respond to the nonshowy, supernatural works of God with a yawn and look desperately for God to speak to us in a showy supernatural manner. "If I could only touch Him, or if He would only touch me, then I could live the Christian life successfully." The tragedy is that as we search for God in "showy" supernatural displays, we overlook His constant supernatural work in us. *We're looking for the trees and miss the forest. We're looking for the supernatural and miss the God of the supernatural.*

That's why Paul repeats himself to the Corinthians: "Do you not know that your body is a temple of the Holy Spirit who is in you, whom you have from God and that you are not your own? For you have been bought with a price; therefore glorify God in your body" (I Corinthians 6:19-20). The same supernatural God that was present in the burning bush before Moses, in the pillar of fire and the cloud that guided the children of Israel and in the holy of holies in the Temple is *in you!* The high priest was only allowed to go into the presence of God in the holy of holies once a year. This was on the Day of Atonement (*Yom Kippur*). He was to offer a sacrifice on that day that would cover the sins of the people for the past year. If he offered the sacrifice wrongly or was himself in a state of sin before God, he would be killed on the spot. As the high priest went into the presence of God he had a rope tied around his foot so that if he was killed, he could be pulled out. The people waited anxiously. When the priest finished his sacrifice and came out, the people breathed a sigh of relief—their sins were covered for another year! The people stood in awe before the presence of God. Now Paul says (with much feeling), "Don't you know that that same presence of God is in you? Now will you act like it?" That's Supernatural Christianity—Naturally!

FOOTNOTES

Chapter 8

1. Maxwell Maltz, *Psycho-Cybernetics* (Hollywood, CA: Wilshire Book Co., 1960), p. 7.
2. Dr. Jay Adams' lecture at Dallas Theological Seminary in 1973.

Nine

WHERE IN THE WORLD IS THE DEVIL?

Having a reputation as a Christian speaker on a college campus, I was called one evening by a student government leader. "Tim, I've got to talk to you tonight!" he blurted out in a panic. I met him at the student center a few minutes later, and nervously, fidgeting, he poured out an incredible story. He had just come from a seance where he had encountered the spirit world face to face. He was obsessed by the voices from the weird meeting, and was he scared. When he finished his tale, I was scared, too.

The next day a girl called. Her roommate was a "white witch" who had read her future from tarot cards. She had told her the name of a young man who would come into her life and bring her good fortune. A few evenings after this prediction, a fiery light appeared to her communicating that it had come to fulfill the prophecy. She ran from the room screaming in terror, afraid to tell anyone what had happened. The next night the fire returned again. Now she was calling me for help.

During that week six different people came to me desperately seeking help. All were oppressed or controlled by forces of the spirit world. All became liberated by applying biblical principles. Since that first week of encountering the spirit world, I've counseled hundreds of people (believers and non-believers) who were bound by the Devil and his evil spirits.

Many believers have unbalanced views concerning the third participant in the Christian life—the Devil. There are two extremes in this area: (1) Ignore him and he'll go away! This extreme believes that the more I know about the Devil the more likely it is that he'll get me. The problem in this extreme is that the Devil is out to get you whether you know about it or not. (2) When in doubt, cast it out! In this extreme nearly everything is blamed on the Devil—including personal sin. This produces spiritual paranoia.

In this chapter Satan's activities of demonization and deception will be set forth. In the following chapter the believer's discernment and defense against Satan will be analyzed and strengthened.

Demonization

There is a great deal of confusion and misunderstanding about the extent of Satan's activity in a believer's life. Much of this perplexity can be alleviated by a proper understanding of the term "demon possession." This term does not appear in the Bible. The word that is translated as demon-possessed is the Greek verb *daimonizomai* which means to be under the power or influence of a demon. Understanding this may make a big difference as to how we answer the question, "Can a Christian be demon-possessed?" If we mean can a Christian be owned by an evil spirit, the answer unquestionably is No. The Christian is owned or possessed by God, for he has been bought with a price (I Corinthians 6:20). If you mean can a Christian be under the power or influence of an evil spirit, the answer assuredly is Yes.

There are three progressive degrees of demonization. Each of these degrees overlaps the next and it is extremely difficult, if not impossible, to discern when one degree of demonization progresses into another.

Harassment

The first degree of demonization is *harassment*. This is the weakest of Satan's attacks. Because he has not been given a place in a person's life through one of his traps, there is very little he can do. At this level he can only thwart or hinder the efforts of believers. He does this by throwing various obstacles in their paths (I Thessalonians 2:18; Romans 15:22). One way he does this is to send destructive and deceptive thoughts into their minds (II Corinthians 10:36; 11:3). Biblical examples of Satan's harassment are the fiery darts in Ephesians 6:16 and the roaring lion metaphor in I Peter 5:8. The chief work of demons in harassment is to throw incessant accusations against a person. A constant barrage of condemning thoughts piles up the guilt so high that the person can't see out.

Influence

The second degree of demonization is *influence*. This has a stronger effect than harassment, for here Satan has been given a place in the believer's life. This usually comes by giving in to or cooperating with Satan's harassment, from believing Satan and not the Lord. At this level the believer is playing right into the enemy's hands, and in some areas can be more influenced by Satan than by the Lord.

Peter clearly illustrates a believer influenced by Satan. After Jesus had experienced an encounter with the Pharisees, He took His disciples across the Sea of Galilee for a time of disciple-building. He taught them about false doctrine, and then He asked them who the people were saying He was. Peter rallied to the occasion by saying, "Thou art the Christ, the Son of the living God" (Matthew 16:16). Jesus commended this answer and revealed His intention to build His Church on the very testimony Peter had just spoken. Then the following conversation between Peter and the Lord took place: "From that time Jesus Christ began to show His disciples that He must go to Jerusalem, and suffer many things from the elders and chief priests and scribes, and be killed, and be raised up on the third day. And Peter took Him aside and began to rebuke Him, saying, 'God forbid it, Lord! This shall never happen to You.' *But He turned and said to Peter, 'Get behind Me, Satan!'*" (Matthew 16:21-23). What a contrast to Peter's previous conversation with Jesus!

We must assume that Jesus knew Peter's name and that this was not simply a slip of the tongue on Jesus' part. I think it's clear that Jesus recognized that Satan was using Peter in an attempt to trap Him. Peter was re-enacting the wilderness temptation—trying to get Jesus to take a short cut to His throne by acting independently from the Father. As soon as He recognized the Satanic influence, Jesus spoke the same words He used in the wilderness—"Get behind Me, Satan!"

Another illustration of believers under the influence of Satan is from Luke 22:31-34. During the last Passover meal, Jesus was teaching the disciples some truths concerning the Kingdom of God and His approaching death. He again foretold His betrayal. But the disciples got into an argument among themselves as to who among them would be the greatest in the Kingdom. This foolish and sinful discussion showed that the disciples were thinking more of themselves than ever before. Jesus rebuked them for their pride. Addressing Peter, He said, "Simon, Simon, behold Satan has demanded permission to sift you like wheat" (Luke 22:31). In other words, Satan wanted to gain influence over these believers, and apparently they had opened the door for him to do so. Jesus went on to explain that this sifting like wheat in Peter's case would be his repeated denial of the Lord.

Control

The third degree of demonization is *control*. This is the strongest degree of attack. A person is normally controlled by

Satanic forces only in certain areas of his life and at certain times, rather than being totally controlled all of the time. Demonic control usually takes place when a person opens one or more areas of his life widely and habitually to evil spirits.

A clear illustration of demonic control is given in Acts 5. Ananias and Sapphira had not confessed their sin to the Lord. Peter asked, "Ananias, why has Satan filled [controlled] your heart to lie to the Holy Spirit, and to keep back some of the price of the land?" (Acts 5:3). Here we see a believer who had the Holy Spirit living in him permanently, yet he was somehow controlled by Satan and made to lie to God.

These three degrees of demonization—harassment, influence and control—span the range of demonic activity in a believer's life. It's impossible for the Devil to demonize a believer beyond the harassment level without the believer himself opening a door through some kind of demonic deception. This is a part of spiritual warfare against the Ultimate Lifestyle.

Deception

Satan is not stupid. He knows that the proverbial red-suited, two-horned, long-tailed, ugly-looking creature with pitchfork in hand, lures few men into his trap. He uses a disguise, concealing his real identity to present himself in a more favorable way. He disguises himself as an "angel of light," appearing to men as a messenger of that which is good and wholesome to imply that he is from God. It was in this way that he approached Jesus in the wilderness. He did not appear to Jesus and offer him something intrinsically bad. He offered him genuinely good things. Behind these good things was the snare—Satan was trying to lure Jesus into acting independently of the Father. That's the Devil-trap: "Do it my way!" Satan is more than willing to give good things, but to obtain them you must do it his way. His way of independence always short-circuits dependence on God and His Word. Satan counterfeits everything that God has to offer—all to trap unsuspecting people.

People everywhere are finding themselves the victims of uncontrollable physical, emotional, and spiritual problems without knowing their sources. Many of these problems are directly or indirectly affected by demonic activity. If the Devil isn't the cause of these problems, he is certainly encouraging and using them. The Bible warns of three major traps that Satan uses—the occult trap, the religious trap, and the sin trap. Every device that Satan uses is a form of one of these traps.

The Occult Trap

"Interest in the occult, for decades the domain of tiny coteries, has suddenly emerged as a mass phenomenon in the United States. Increasing thousands of Americans are now active practitioners of witchcraft, spiritualism, magic, and even devil worship. Millions more are addicted to astrology, numerology, fortune-telling and tarot cards."[1] Most people view this mass phenomenon as intriguing and harmless, but there are some who are convinced that occult practices are not so harmless.

Dr. Kurt E. Koch recognizes the coincidence between psychic disturbance and occult participation. He points out: "The neurosis epidemic corresponds on the counseling level to the post-war flood of psychical disturbances, which in many observed instances stand in noteworthy frequency ratio to the increasing occult practices. 'Insecure' man seeks in every manner to escape the growing unknown about the fact of his dear ones, about the threatening future, about health, and about mere existence, and consequently takes recourse for help to occult manipulation."[2] Dr. William S. Reed, a U.S. psychiatrist, says, "Many mental and physical illnesses result, in fact, from demonic attacks."[3] Even within the occult camp there is concern over the serious effects people are experiencing from participation in the occult. The quarterly magazine

Occult, in its first edition of 1973, included an article entitled "Why I Started a Psychic Rescue Squad," which discusses severe problems caused directly by occult activity.

The Bible also convinces us that the occult is dangerous and warns of tampering with any part of it. The Lord makes it clear that He hates occult practices. In Deuteronomy 18:9-13 He lists various activities of the occult and says He finds them detestable: "Thou shalt not learn to do after the abominations of these nations. There shall not be found with thee any one . . . that useth divination [fortune-teller], or an observer of the times [soothsayer], or an enchanter [magician], or a witch [sorceress], or a charmer [hypnotist], or a consulter with familiar spirits [medium controlled by a spirit], or a wizard [clairvoyant or psychic], or a necromancer [medium who consults the dead]. For all that do these things are an abomination to the Lord" (KJV).

The word "occult" refers to things covered over, mysterious, concealed, or hidden. The occult goes beyond human understanding and the five senses. In every occult experience there is contact with the spirit world, to which there is an appeal for some hidden knowledge of the past or future and/or an experience of power. The spirit world does not consist of spirits of the dead, but of angelic beings—both good and bad. The bad spirits that are linked with the occult are fallen angels who followed Lucifer's (Satan's) rebellion and remained in subjection to him" (Matthew 12:24). Satan uses his army of spirits (demons) to carry out his wicked strategy. Ephesians 6:11-12 indicates an organized system within the ranks of demons possibly involving assignment of demons to specific individuals so that they can know a person fully, including his or her weaknesses and strengths. This could explain the incredibly intimate knowledge a "spirit of a departed loved one" reveals in a seance. It is not the spirit of the dead person speaking, but a demon who knew the person very well.

Many people caught up in the occult tell how they crave the power, knowledge, and feeling it gives: "I desire it, but it scares me so!" Linda was one example, a single working girl who had always been fascinated with the occult. She found herself controlled by a spirit after yielding through an emotional crisis in her life. Linda had been notified that her fiancé David had been killed in action in Viet Nam. A few days later she received a poem from David which he had written just before his death. Naturally she cherished it, and after consulting the ouija board, decided to tack it on the inside of her closet door.

Within a week Linda revealed to her roommates that David's spirit lived in her closet: "He tells me what to do and what not to do. I like it, but for some reason he scares me!" The roommates brushed this aside as pure fantasizing caused by her grief, until one evening they found Linda shaking with fear from what David's spirit had told her to do. Immediately all three girls consulted the ouija board: it said that Linda should burn the poem. Understandably, she vehemently refused to burn the last word from her lover, and finally when she had calmed down, they all retired for the night.

About 12:20 A.M. her roommates heard a terrible scream from Linda's bedroom. They rushed in, turned on the light, and stood in shock at the scene—the closet door had been ripped off its hinges! It was an incredible sight! That changed Linda's mind in a hurry. She jumped out of bed and burned the poem. Now Linda will tell you that David's spirit lives inside her: "He tells me what to do and what not to do. I like it, but it scares me so!"

The occult is remarkably fascinating, yet this fascination is a trap set by Satan and his evil spirits. No matter how good it looks, how appealing it is, or how harmless it seems, the occult is dangerous. Millions of people have opened themselves up to the powers of darkness through their fascination with the occult.

The Religious Trap

This is by far Satan's most effective trap. Because it is wrapped in a religious package, it has both the benefits of the alluring power of the occult and the respectability of the religious. Many people would not think of tampering with the occult, but if a persuasive leader puts a religious cloak over it, claims it is from God and quotes some Bible verses, they become victims of the religious trap.

Paul warns that "in later times some will fall away from the faith, paying attention to deceitful spirits and doctrines of demons" (I Timothy 4:1). He strikes at the energizing source behind false teachers—the subtle deception of false doctrine which comes from Satan's evil spirits. The Bible presents four significant characteristics of the false teachers through which the evil spirits do their work of deceiving. All of these characteristics might not be found in any one person.

(1) *False teachers profess to be believers.* Paul says of them: "For such men are false apostles, deceitful workers, disguising themselves as apostles of Christ. And no wonder, for even Satan disguises himself as an angel of light. Therefore it is not surprising if his servants also disguise themselles as servants of righteousness; whose end shall be according to their deeds" (II Corinthians 11:13-15). These are not men who consciously worship the Devil while pretending to be servants of righteousness. They actually believe they are servants of righteousness because of the deception of the spirits.

(2) *False Teachers act in the name of Jesus.* "Many will say to Me [Jesus] on that day, 'Lord, Lord, did we not prophesy in Your name, and in Your name cast out demons, and in Your name perform many miracles?' (Matthew 7:22). Their first claim is that they have spoken and even predicted in Jesus' name. Jesus warns us: "Beware of the false prophets, who come to you in sheep's clothing, but inwardly are ravenous wolves" (Matthew 7:15). Speaking in the name of the Lord is part of the "sheep's clothing" that disguises "ravenous wolves."

The second claim false teachers make in their defense is that they cast out demons in the name of the Lord Jesus. Many people use this as conclusive evidence that a person's work is of the Lord, supporting their belief with Jesus' words to the Pharisees in Matthew 12. The Pharisees had accused Him of casting out demons by the power of Satan. Jesus replied, "If Satan casts out Satan, he is divided against himself; how then shall his kingdom stand?" (Matthew 12:26). At first glance the words of Jesus do seem to suggest that Satan would not cast out one of his evil spirits, but this is not the whole picture. He would not cast out his evil spirits if it would cause him permanent damage, but he would if it could, in any way, further his influence and power. He will use even that which seems harmful to himself if it will eventually extend his control.

I am convinced that much casting out of demons we witness today does no more than open the door to more extensive demonic control in a person's life. The release is only temporary.

The final claim made by false teachers here is that they perform many miracles in the name of Jesus. Jesus warns us that in the last days before He returns to the earth "false prophets will arise and will show great signs and wonders, so as to mislead, if possible, even the elect" (Matthew 24:24).

Through the deception of Satan, false teachers may receive occult powers unknowingly, believing these powers are the supernatural gift of God. An excellent example of this is a Mexican peasant woman I interviewed. Carlita first noticed she possessed healing power when she was able to cure animals in the circus where she worked. This had continued for some time before she became aware that a spirit by the name of Hermanito Cuauhtemoc was working through her. He explained to Carlita that he had been sent by God to heal people through her. She accepted the opportunity to be used by God in this way, and Cuauhtemoc has now been healing people through Carlita for nearly fifty years.

Carlita's healings are strange. She does not pray over individuals asking God to heal them—she actually operates on them with a dull hunting knife. She has performed every kind of operation imaginable—on the heart, the back, the eyes, etc. A medical doctor who had observed Carlita perform many operations was present when I interviewed her. He told of one case where Carlita cut into a person's chest cavity, took the heart out for examination, allowed the doctor to handle it. After she had closed the person up, without stitches, she suggested that he go to his hotel room and rest for three days. When the three days were up he left Mexico City, a healthy man, with no scars from the surgery. I asked the doctor what explanation he could give for such an amazing work. He replied: "There is no explanation medically. It's a miracle!"

The remarkable thing about Carlita's work is that she always operates in a dark room with her eyes shut. The reason is that Carlita does not do the operations herself—Hermanito Cuauhtemoc acts through her. When he takes over her body, her eyes close and he speaks and acts through her. He has total control.

Carlita's ministry comes from a sincere heart. She gives all of the glory to God, who she believes sent Cuauhtemoc to work these mighty acts of power through her. Nevertheless, she is being deceived. Carlita is a medium by her own admission, and it is Cuauhtemoc who is in control, not the Lord. He claims to be the spirit of the ancient Aztec Indian chief who now is chief of all the spirits in North America. He was sent by his "god" all right, Satan, the god of the world. Carlita is deceived by the false belief that everything supernatural must be from God, especially if it helps people. After talking with Carlita for two hours, and listening to Cuauhtemoc twice during the evening, I asked her the source of her power. She answered, "If not God, who else?"

Satan is the most effective counterfeiter the world will ever know. He loves to give good experiences that make people feel spiritually high or to give them a sense of supernatural power working in and through them—all in the name of Jesus!

(3) *False teachers will have many followers.* A popular, though incorrect, way to measure God's blessing is the "numbers game." Just because a teacher has many followers is not conclusive evidence that God approves. Jesus warned, "And many false prophets [teachers] will arise, and will mislead many" (Matthew 24:11). Peter echoed the same warning:

"There will also be false teachers among you, who will secretly introduce destructive heresies. . . . And many will *follow* their sensuality" (II Peter 2:1-2). Many will follow the false teachers because of the clever disguise the angel of light has cast upon them. Numbers alone do not constitute a valid test of whether a ministry is of God, because Satan's deceptive work will also produce a great following.

(4) *False teachers place God's Word secondary to experience.* This general characteristic is common in the religious trap. The Bible is viewed as a primer, but experience is ultimate. People accept their supernatural experiences as gifts from God without any scriptural basis for them. The Bible constantly warns us not to pay attention to anything or anybody not in agreement with the revealed Word. Isaiah warns: "To the law and to the testimony! If they do not speak according to this word [Word of God], it is because they have no dawn [light]" (Isaiah 8:20).

The Lord will not guide men into anything that is contrary to or in addition to the Bible. Paul cautions us "not to exceed what is written" (I Corinthians 4:6), and John tells us to watch ourselves, for "anyone who goes too far and does not abide in the teaching of Christ does not have God; the one who abides in the teaching, he has both the Father and the Son" (II John:9).

Although he speaks specifically about false teachers, John's words can also be applied to false experiences. If your supernatural experience does not match up to the Word of God, then it is time to test it out. Satan loves nothing more than to give people overwhelming and thrilling experiences that seem to come from God. This is all part of his disguise as an angel of light to snare people in the religious trap. Many unsuspecting believers have sought something deeper from the Lord, have received visions, obtained powers, and gifts— all coming from the Counterfeiter instead.

The Sin Trap

The effects of this trap are universal, because all have

sinned. Sin in its most fundamental sense is opposition to God, to Adam's sin of rebellion against God's specified plan. Man is sinful by nature. It isn't necessary to teach a child to lie or to rebel against authority—he will do these things naturally.

Satan is not only the originator of sin, he is also the minister of it. Everything that opposes God's commandments aligns itself with him. Sin is his business. He works to lure people's thoughts, attitudes, and actions into rebellion against God. The Devil's work further consists of accusing people of their sin and forcing them to believe they must pay for it themselves. "The god of this world [Satan] has blinded the minds of the unbelieving, that they might not see the light of the gospel" (II Corinthians 4:4).

The light of the gospel is the fact that Jesus has already paid for man's sin. He came to destroy the activity of Satan. "The Son of God appeared for this purpose, that He might destroy the works of the devil" (I John 3:8). How could those works be destroyed? The penalty for man's sin is death, and Jesus died on the cross, paying that penalty for everyone. By simply accepting Christ's payment for sin, anyone can experience forgiveness and freedom from its penalty.

All of this is a free gift to you (Romans 6:23), but a gift is not yours to enjoy until you personally accept it. This acceptance is what Jesus meant by the word "believe." He put it simply when He said, "For God so loved the world that He gave His only begotten Son [Jesus], that whoever believes in Him should not perish [will not have to pay the death penalty for his own sin], but have eternal life [right now]" (John 3:16). A person who recognizes himself or herself as a sinner, and acknowledges his or her need to make payment for that sin, is in a perfect position to accept personally Christ's payment.

We see that the unbeliever has no choice but to be enslaved by sin because he has not chosen to accept Christ's gift of freedom from sin. On the other hand, the believer can choose whether he will operate in rebellion against God, or whether he will act from his newborn spirit to obey God. As long as the believer acts from his newborn spirit, he enjoys his personal relationship with God through Christ. When he acts in sin, he is robbed of the enjoyment of that relationship. John tells us that in order to enjoy our relationship with God after we have sinned, we must simply confess, humbly acknowledge our sins to Him. We cannot lose our relationship with the Lord; yet we may often lose the enjoyment of it.

The sin trap involves neglect of this practice of confession or acknowledgement of sin in the believer's life. It's clear from Scripture that habitual sin opens the door to demonic attack in the believer's life. Sin may be defined simply as disobedience to the revealed will of God either by commission—a voluntary action, or by omission—an act of neglect. Its basic intent opposes God. A believer who sins acts against God and in favor of the Devil, and when he is involved in habitual or unconfessed sin, he is playing right into the hands of the Enemy. Satan will take advantage of him (II Corinthians 2:11).

In the middle of a paragraph dealing with habitual sin, Paul says: "Be angry, and yet do not sin; do not let the sun go down on your anger, and do not give the Devil an opportunity [a place]" (Ephesians 4:26-27). Paul strongly states that Satan's activity in a believer's life is triggered by habitual and unacknowledged sin.

Many times a believer is unaware of how habitual sin opens the door to demonic activity and through ignorance fully cooperates with Satan. After harboring the sin for a period of time, the believer will come to a point where he is truly repentant and will confess the sin to God. A few days later he may find himself committing the same sin. He confesses it again. The cycle goes on—sin, confess, sin, confess, sin. . . . He becomes frustrated and defeated and begins to wonder how he can do such a thing. He questions whether he's really a believer or not. Depression sets in and he is spiritually defeated.

There are at least two reasons why this believer has been wiped out. The first is that he may have a faulty understanding of the spiritual life and the implications of Christ's victory over sin. But the second is just as destructive and even more subtle—he may be ignorant of Satan's devices. If Satan has trapped him through his sin, he can confess until he's blue in the face—and he probably will—but the trap will not be released. Confession only deals with sin committed wilfully. He must deal with Satan himself in order to get out of the sin trap. If I were being choked by a bully right now, I wouldn't start beating my own leg to make him quit. I would attack the bully.

Satan tricks people into believing his activity is nothing more than the product of sin in their own defeated lives. It is true that people do sin habitually, and the sin itself must be dealt with. But Satan may have slipped into the open door provided by the sin to gain a foothold in the believer's life, and he must be handled as well. This is the kind of sin trap that results in uncontrollable spiritual problems.

Jerry is a good illustration of a believer caught in the sin trap. He just could not gain the victory over his sinful problem—homosexuality. The filthy thought and periodically the act itself was dragging him into suicidal depression. It seemed like the more he fought the problem the worse it became. Just a few days before he came in for counseling he said he actually felt "driven" to a park to participate in homosexuality. This problem had definitely become uncontrollable, and he was afraid of what he might do next. He said, "If this is how I must live the rest of my days, I might as well end my life!" I agreed with him. That night we dealt not only with Jerry's sin of yielding to homosexuality, but also with the demonic problem that was present because of his sin. It was exciting to witness a young man, deep in sin and enslaved by evil spirits, freed by the power of the Lord Jesus Christ.

When the sin trap is unveiled with all its devastation, sin is seen to be a more serious matter than we thought. We should not become paranoid about it, but we should become more sensitive to sin's power. Playing with sin is not a spiritual game. It's opening the door to a fierce enemy, Satan—who plays for keeps. Through the activities of demonization and deception the Devil sets out to destroy us. Now let's see what we can do to the Devil!

FOOTNOTES

Chapter 9

1. "The Cult of the Occult," *Newsweek*, April 13, 1970, p. 96.
2. Kurt E. Koch, *Christian Counseling and Occultism* (Grand Rapids, MI: Kregel Publications, 1972) p. 22.
3. Kurt E. Koch, *Occult Bondage and Deliverance* (Grand Rapids, MI: Kregel Publications, 1970), vol. I, p. 15.

Ten

SCARING THE HELL OUT OF THE DEVIL!

There are three very basic principles in warfare which, when violated, lead to sure defeat. The first is realizing that a war is going on. The soldier who sits in his barracks while they are being bombed, refusing to believe in the reality of war is in big trouble. The second principle is knowing the enemy's methods and strategies. The great militarists have always been faithful students of their enemies. They knew that neglect in this area would almost guarantee defeat. The third principle is knowing how to fight. A man can be certain that he is in battle and know all there is to know about his enemy, but if he doesn't know how to fight, he's headed for destruction.

Many believers in Christ, who already have the promise of victory over the Enemy, are experiencing daily defeats in their spiritual warfare. Most of these defeats result from ignorance of one of the three basic principles of warfare. First, some Christians ignore the reality of spiritual war. A tragic number of believers are under the impression that spiritual warfare only involves the battle of their old sinful nature against their new nature in Christ. These believers have one thing in common—they are defeated in their daily experience by demonic activity. Second, many Christians do not know Satan's methods and stategies. Although Scripture has a lot to say about the person and work of Satan, believers are extremely ignorant about him. Satan's devices are not always filthy or frightening in appearance, nor are they always obvious as many imagine. Third, believers are ignorant of their role in spiritual warfare against the devices of their enemy. The question that puzzles the believer is "How do I fight the spiritual war?" Now that we have discussed Satan's strategies of deception we must attempt to answer this question.

Two statements of caution are necessary in approaching this explosive subject. Both are found in Christ's words to His disciples. At the beginning of Luke 10 we read that the Lord appointed seventy men to go ahead of Him and minister in the cities. They returned from their journey rejoicing, especially about the power over demons they had in using Christ's name. "And the seventy returned with joy, saying, 'Lord, even the demons are subject to us in Your name.' And He said to them, 'I was watching Satan fall from heaven like lightning. Behold, I have given you authority to tread upon serpents and scorpions, and over all the power of the enemy, and nothing shall injure you.' " Then Jesus brought the situation into perspective by saying, "Nevertheless do not rejoice in this, that the spirits are subject to you, but rejoice that your names are recorded in heaven" (Luke 10:17-20).

The two cautions are: (1) *Be careful of becoming a "demon inspector."* It's very easy to diagnose half your friends and all your enemies as having a demonic problem. The demon inspector is continually looking for a demonic explanation of adversity, forgetting that many problems and weird happenings occur that are not caused by Satan and his demons. (2) *Be careful of becoming demon-centered rather than Christ-centered.* The subject of demon activity is exciting. This excitement can spread rapidly. The believer must not allow the subject of Satan and his devices to occupy more of his thought and conversation than Christ and His work of salvation do.

Discernment

There is much bewilderment today about testing the

spirits—discerning what is of God and what is of Satan. The purpose in this is not simply to distinguish "evil" spirits from "good" spirits—there is more than that involved. The testing in itself can be a trick of the Devil, for we know that Satan sends out many "good" spirits. We must test to distinguish all spirits from the Holy Spirit. John R. W. Stott, in his commentary *The Epistles of John*, presents an excellent balance here. He says: "There is an urgent need for discernment among Christians. We are often too gullible, and exhibit a naive readiness to credit messages and teachings which purport to come from the spirit world. There is such a thing, however, as a misguided charity and tolerance toward false doctrine. Unbelief (believe not every spirit) which can be as much a mark of spiritual maturity as belief. *We need to preserve the biblical balance, avoiding on the one hand the extreme superstition which believes everything and on the other extreme suspicion which believes nothing.*"[1]

Four basic tests are given in the Bible to discern Satan's spirits, whether they are "good" or "bad," from the Holy Spirit. The first three are specific tests meant to confront the spirits directly. The last is a more general test, but is still very significant.

The first test is based on this truth: "Every spirit that confesses that Jesus Christ has come in the flesh is from God" (I -John 4:2). The Holy Spirit acknowledges the incarnation of the Lord Jesus—that He was a real man as well as God.

The second test is from Paul's instructions to the Corinthians: "Therefore I make known to you, that no one speaking by the Spirit of God says, 'Jesus is accursed'; and no one can say 'Jesus is Lord,' except by the Holy Spirit" (I Corinthians 12:3). This test revolves around acknowledgment of the Lordship of Jesus Christ. An evil spirit knows that Jesus is the Lord, but will never confess Him as *his* Lord. His lord is Satan. Satan encourages talk and activity about Jesus, but not about the Lord Jesus Christ. I become suspicious of groups who are always speaking of Jesus, but hardly ever speak of Him as the Lord Jesus.

The third test is acknowledgment that the shed blood of the Lord Jesus has power to cleanse from sin—the evil spirit will deny this (I John 5:6-7). We are told that Christ came "that He might destroy the works of the devil" (I John 3:8). He did this when He shed His blood on the cross (Colossians 2:15). That is why Revelation 12:11 proclaims that believers overcome Satan "by the blood of the Lamb." A devotee of Hare Krishna had been busy chanting when the blood of the Lord Jesus Christ was mentioned. He literally jumped up and ran in fear! This young man responded to the blood of Christ just as an evil spirit would, and although he did not give us a chance to question him, his immediate reaction spoke very loudly.

These three specific tests involve confronting the spirit directly. In other words, we are testing the spirit, not the person affected by the spirit. In many cases the spirit must be in operation in order to test it. An illustration of this is the case of a woman who had "received the gift of speaking in tongues." She was challenged to test the spirit that spoke through her lips to see if her new gift was from God. To put the woman under these three tests would have been futile. She acknowledged the incarnation, the Lordship, and the blood sacrifice of the Lord Jesus. The spirit she had received had to be tested in an altogether different way. While she prayed in tongues, another person prayed and tested the spirit that was operating through her at that moment. The spirit went into a rage and acknowledged that his lord was Satan. (This is not meant to imply that all tongues are from the Devil. There are three sources of tongues—God, Satan, and psychological.)

The fourth test is that the Holy Spirit acknowledges *only* what is biblical, while an evil spirit moves away from the Word in two directions—toward extra-biblical and non-biblical activity. Extra-biblical experiences and teachings "go beyond that which is written" (I Corinthians 4:6). The non-biblical experiences involve the misuse of biblical teaching through misinterpretation, misapplication, and overemphasis. Satan is delighted when the Bible is misused. Believers must be careful not to get off on tangents in their Bible study, centering their lives on things other than Christ. Since the main purpose in the Christian life is to become more like the Lord Jesus, it is extremely important that believers diligently seek Christlikeness and maturity over everything else.

The fifth and final test could be called biblical discernment. Testing spirits involves spiritual discernment, and this comes only from God's Word. Paul says that "he who is spiritual discerns all things" (I Corinthians 2:15).

Defense

After finishing a session on resisting the Devil, a new believer blurted out, "Well, in plain English you're telling us how to scare the hell out of the Devil, right?" No plainer words were ever spoken! We must learn to resist the Devil. James, Peter, and Paul all command us to resist him, but very few people understand what that means. It's important to realize that fighting the spiritual warfare is a natural part of the Christian lifestyle—an everyday occurrence. It must be viewed as routine.

Resisting is not the same as casting out demons. It's interesting to note that casting out demons is reported throughout the Gospels, but it is not mentioned in the Epistles. In the Epistles we are taught to resist Satan personally. This is not to deny that demons may be cast out today. Certainly there are cases in which Satan's control is so great that demons must be cast out or exorcized. However, to approach every demonic problem that way is unwise and can be dangerous to spiritual and mental health. The teaching of the New Testament is that the believer is to resist Satan. Therefore, he should be taught how to do this, to enable him successfully to fight the spiritual war so that he will not be forced into dependence on a neighborhood exorcist.

Reckoning

There is more to resisting Satan than telling him, "Get

lost in the name of Jesus." Resisting rests upon two pillars; without them resisting is futile. The first pillar is reckoning. This is the believer's offense in the battle front within—the flesh. To resist means to stand, to stand as victor, to stand invincibly, to stand successfully. On what are we to stand? We are to stand on the victory won at the cross, for in that victory Christ "delivered us from the domain of darkness, and transferred us to the kingdom of His beloved Son" (Colossians 1:13). We must stand on our position of being in Christ, united with Him in His death and resurrection. Since we are in Christ, and He has all authority in heaven and earth, we are in the only place of victory, standing "in the Lord and in the strength of His might" (Ephesians 6:10).

The very nature of our spiritual armor shows that we stand as victors. Every piece of the armor of God is defensive, with the possible exception of the sword. Because the victory has already been won, we need simply to stand our ground. Satan has been defeated at the cross (Colossians 2:8-15) and made powerless (Hebrews 2:14-15)—he has no right in any area of the believer's life. The believer needs to stand on what is his in Christ. He does not need to attack, but to stand as a victor.

Peter's teaching on resisting reinforces this picture of standing. Remember that Peter had been sifted like wheat and used by Satan to trap the Lord Jesus. Peter knew what could happen. With his experience behind him, he was certain to warn other believers of the Devil's schemes. In I Peter, he expresses his confidence in a verse that is often quoted: "Casting all your anxiety upon Him, because He cares for you" (I Peter 5:7). This is an outstanding truth to share in a short devotional, but most believers stop here and relax. Peter doesn't. He immediately takes believers out of the clouds, and shouts a warning in the next two verses: "Be of sober spirit, be on the alert. Your adversary, the devil, prowls about like a roaring lion, seeking someone to devour. But resist him, firm in your faith" (I Peter 5:8-9). Peter says we should be on the lookout because the Enemy, Satan, is a fierce destroyer out to get believers. He uses a term here which means to be as solid as a rock. This is definitely appropriate coming from Peter, whose name meant "The Rock."

Unless we reckon on our position in Christ (dead to the flesh, but alive to God), we have nothing on which to stand. Without reckoning ourselves dead to the flesh, we will slip back down under the control of the flesh and its lusts, constantly opening the door to Satan's accusations. Without reckoning ourselves to be alive to God, we can never enjoy the confidence and security of experiencing our life in Christ and standing victoriously. In Christ we have authority to resist Satan, for it is in Christ that all authority in heaven and earth lies. Unless we reckon on our position in Christ there is no power available to us from His sacrificial death to overcome the Devil (Revelation 12:11). We cannot resist without reckoning.

Renewing

The second pillar that supports resisting is renewing. This is the believer's action against the battlefront without—the world. In Ephesians Paul clearly tells us that we must put on armor to resist Satan: "Put on the full armor of God, that you may be able to stand firm against the schemes of the devil. . . . Therefore, take up the full armor of God, that you may be able to resist in the evil day, and having done everything, to stand firm. Stand firm therefore . . ." (6:11, 13, 14). "Having done everything" means having finished putting on God's armor. Without renewing the mind through the Word of God, a believer will not have the power or ability to resist Satan. There is no resisting without renewing.

Resisting without reckoning and renewing is a farce— and Satan knows it! If only believers were convinced of this how different the spiritual war would be! Instead of hearing Satan's ridiculous laughter at our futile resistance, we would be hearing the fleeing footsteps of a defeated foe. We have the promise that if we resist him properly, Satan must flee (James 4:7). *This proper resistance includes reckoning—acting against the flesh—, renewing—acting against the world, and then resisting—acting against Satan.* Proper resistance will indeed "scare the hell out of the devil!"

FOOTNOTES

Chapter 10

1. John R. W. Stott, *The Epistles of John* (Grand Rapids, MI: Wm. B. Eerdmans Pub. Co., 1966), pp. 153.

Part Three

POSITION—WHERE IS THE ULTIMATE LIFESTYLE LIVED?

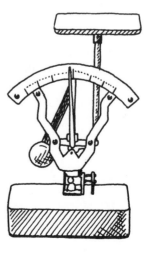

Eleven

A TIME TO OBEY— A TIME TO DISOBEY

Where is the Christian life lived? Right where the Christian lives—*in the world!* It's not above, below, beyond, or in isolation from the world—it's in the world. The fact that the Christian lives out his life in the world poses two questions: (1) How do I relate to the world? and (2) How do I relate the good news to the world? The second question will be discussed in the following chapter. The answer to the first question rests on a proper understanding of authority—the realms of authority, the rationale of authority, and a balanced response to authority.

Extreme approaches to authority range from absolute freedom from all authority to a position of being a kind of holy doormat. The latter extreme—total obedience and submission—has risen to frightening dimensions within the body of Christ. It has permeated Christian teaching to the point where some believe that God only works through a "chain of command," and Satan only attacks when a believer is not properly situated within the chain.

The whole issue of authority has been emphasized to extreme and elevated to an unwarranted position in the Christian life. The result is confusion to the point of spiritual paralysis and unnecessary pain as some beautiful gems have been shattered by the "hammer and chisel" effect. The confusion and the pain can be cleared up, but only by proper focus on authority—the realization that there is a time to obey and a time to disobey.

Realms of Authority

There are five general realms of authority revealed in the Bible. The first is *government*. This realm is discussed most extensively by Paul in Romans 13:1-7 and I Timothy 2:1-7 and by Peter in I Peter 2:13-17. The primary function of government is "the punishment of evil-doers and the praise of those who do right" (I Peter 2:14). The second realm is that of *employment*. Paul speaks of this in Colossians 3:22-26 and Ephesians 6:5-9, and Peter in I Peter 2:18-19. The third realm of authority is the *church*. Here elders are to be set up in authority to direct and shepherd the flock of God. The position of elder is discussed in I and II Timothy, Titus, and I Peter 5:1-5. Elders who function well in this position will receive a special reward from the Lord Jesus at His coming—a crown of glory (I Peter 5:4). The fourth realm of authority is the *marriage relationship*. The most exhaustive treatments of this relationship are found in Ephesians 5:22-33 and I Peter 3:1-7. Because of the day-to-day struggles which are involved in this intimate relationship, it is the realm which receives the most attention. The fifth realm of authority is the *parent-child relationship*. Paul is the only New Testament writer who addresses himself to this area of authority. He discusses it briefly in Ephesians 6:1-4 and Colossians 3:20-21.

Rationale of Authority

The source of all authority is God. "There is no authority except from God, and those which exist are established by God" (Romans 13:1). Only God holds absolute authority. Therefore, every person or institution, other than God, which is functioning within a given realm of authority only possesses relative authority. It is never absolute.

Being in authority then does not mean having absolute authority; neither does it mean being better than another person. Authority carries no connotation of one person being better or greater than another. Not long ago I was on my way to speak at a local university, and as I was running late, I was moving across the city rather swiftly. I was only two blocks away from the campus when a man walked out in the middle of the street and put his hand in the air signaling me to stop. I came to a screeching halt. Now, I didn't stop because I thought this guy was better than I was, or because I thought he could beat me up. I stopped because he was wearing a little tin badge on his shirt—he was a policeman! That impressed me to stop. He had authority.

God has set up a *line of authority* within each realm of authority. The purpose of this line is threefold, and each purpose builds on the other. The primary purpose of the line of authority is to *counteract chaos*. It's to give orderliness so people can get things done.

A few years ago five of us began a new organization. Since none of us wanted any of the rest to be the head of the organization, we decided that we would function as a unified leadership. That sounded great (even a bit spiritual), but because we had no line of authority our new organization immediately deteriorated into disorganization. Our various responsibilities overlapped to the point that everyone felt overly responsibile or irresponsible. We met for hours to decide on such major issues as how many phones we should have, how much stationery we needed, and when we should have our next meeting. When we took a vote, it would come out 3 to 2, or on rare occasions was 4 to 1. (That one was easy. We just ignored the guy for a few days, and he would come around.) Believe me, we experienced nothing but chaos until we set up a line of authority. Every relationship that sets out to accomplish something must follow a line of authority in order to get the job done smoothly. It's the oil of human relationships.

The other two purposes for the line of authority build upon the foundation of counteracting chaos: *to create an atmosphere for a quiet life of godliness* and *to communicate the good news of God to non-believers*. Paul speaks of these in his first letter to Timothy. "I urge that entreaties and prayers, petitions and thanksgivings, be made on behalf of all men, for kings and *all who are in authority, in order that we may lead a tranquil and quiet life in all godliness and dignity*" (I Timothy 2:1-2). Communication of the good news results naturally in an atmosphere of quiet godliness. Paul continues, "This is good and acceptable in the sight of God our Savior, *who desires all men to be saved and to come to the knowledge of the truth*" (I Timothy 2:3-4). Peter gives the same reason for following the governmental line of authority, "Keep your behavior excellent among the Gentiles [non-believers], so that in the thing in which they slander you as evil-doers, they may on account of your good deeds, as they observe them, glorify God" (I Peter 2:12). The line of authority is set up by God for the purpose of counteracting chaos (produced by the Fall of man), which will create the necessary atmosphere for a quiet life of godliness and will enable the good news of God to be communicated to the non-believing world.

Response to Authority

In the light of the fact that God is the source of all authority and has established a line of authority through given realms or spheres, what should our response be? The balanced view for the Ultimate Lifestyle is that there is a time to obey and a time to disobey.

A Time to Obey!

In discerning what time it is (to obey or disobey), it is crucial to begin by understanding a precept (absolute law) and a principle (absolute guideline) concerning authority. Dr.

Grant Howard, in his excellent book *Knowing God's Will and Doing It!*, distinguished between a precept and a principle in this way: "precepts are specific, detailed instructions as to what God wants the believer to do and not to do. . . . Principles are general directions that must be applied to specific situations. The sign that reads *SPEED LIMIT 25 MPH* is a precept. The sign that reads *DRIVE CAREFULLY* is a principle. I apply the latter in one way in heavy traffic and in another way on a deserted street."[1] *The precept of authority is that God has absolute authority and must be obeyed absolutely.* No other authority is over Him, and there is no other authority without Him. The believer must always obey God.

The principle of authority is total submission (obedience) up to the point of personal sin (disobedience against God). The believer must obey the constituted authority up to the point where it directs something which would be disobedient to God.

A Time to Disobey!

There are at least three conditions in which we may or must disobey a constituted authority. *The first is when the authority figure is no longer your authority.* The most common illustration of this is in the parent-child relationship. As long as a child is dependent upon his parents financially, he is under their authority. In today's culture there are two ways that children are removed from that parental authority. One is by their establishing single independent status, and the other is by their creating a separate unit through marriage. Both remove them from the parental authority by moving them out of the financially dependent relationship. In both types of independence the child must still honor his parents (value them and their advice), but he is not bound to obey them. "Children or dependent ones obey your parents!" "Every one honor your parents!" The line between obeying and honoring is very clear. You step over it when you leave the dependent state.

The second condition in which we may or must disobey is

when the authority figure takes over another realm of authority. There are numerous illustrations of this condition. One that is all too common is the feeling within Christian groups that all men are in authority over all women. This is simply not true. The fact that a man is in authority (not better than, but responsible for) in his own home over his wife does not imply that he is in authority over all women. Another example is the case of governmental authority stepping into the parental authority realm and attempting to become the parent, or of governmental authority intruding in the realm of church authority, directing a church not to meet. We may disobey here in such cases.

The third condition is when the authority figure directs us to sin against God. This condition overrides the other two and is really the crux of the issue of a proper response to authority. Any time another authority directs us to do something that is against the revealed will of the Lord we may disobey.

It is very important that the right process be followed when disobedience seems necessary. The following are six suggestions for this process: (1) *Pray for change.* When you have been directed to sin against God, pray for a change in the situation. Pray that either the authority figure removes the directive, or that the authority figure is removed.

(2) *Evaluate the directive.* About five years ago I spoke to a ladies' Thursday morning Bible study. After I finished, a woman came up to me and said, "I'm sure you'll agree with me when I say that God really wanted me here this morning." I waited for her explanation. "You see, my husband has made it very clear that he doesn't want me coming here anymore, but you and I both know that the Bible is filled with Scripture concerning our need for attending such groups as this." I asked if she could find me one of those Scriptures. She sat down and searched through her Bible for a verse indicating she should attend Thursday morning Bible study. After searching in vain she said, "Do you know any?" "No," I replied, "I don't believe I've ever read anything like that in the Bible." She said, "Well, what do you think I should do?"

"That's easy," I said, "I think you should stay home on Thursday mornings." She squirmed a bit, "But what would God think?" I smiled and said, "I think He would be impressed." Going to Thursday morning Bible study is not an absolute in God's revelation. It's not a sin against God to miss it. We must be careful to evaluate whether or not the directive is actually sin and not use God as an excuse to exercise our own rebellion against it.

(3) *Seek an alternative to disobedience.* If after careful evaluation of the directive, you come to the decision that it is commanding you to sin, then seek to discover the real reason why the authority figure made the directive. There might be a way to meet the basic intent of the directive without sinning by suggesting an alternative. For instance, let's say that your mate wants to swap mates—to do a little swinging. Obviously, this is against God's revelation, but what is the real reason your mate would suggest such a thing? Maybe it's because your mate is bored with you sexually. Because it aims at the real reason behind the directive, a successful alternative in this case might be to overwhelm your mate sexually.

A very common illustration of this is when the husband directs the wife not to attend church. It's easy to show that God's Word states the necessity for participation in the body of believers, and although an occasional absence would certainly not be sin, never participating in the body would be. I've had eleven cases of this in the counseling center over the past five years, and in every case there was an underlying need or reason behind the husband's directive. Usually the wife had set up a pulpit ministry in the home, and the husband was getting tired of listening to her. The husband's reasoning was, "I must shut off the supply of religious information, so she won't be able to preach to me!"

Realizing that this was the real reason behind the husbands' directives, I suggested to each wife that she attack her predicament by an alternative to disobedience. I advised her to "retire" from the pulpit ministry in the home—quit preaching at him—and stay home for about a month. Then I suggested asking him at that point if he minded her going to church. In every case the husband then thought it was fine for his wife to go. In fact, in two cases the husbands were upset with their wives for *not* going over the past few weeks. They had forgotten the reason they didn't want them to go.

(4) *Pray for wisdom and boldness*. When you've taken the first three suggested steps and the directive is still not relieved, pray for wisdom and boldness to know how and when to disobey.

(5) *Maintain a godly spirit as you disobey*. This is no time for a hot temper, abusive accusations, or bitter reactions. It's a time for a sincere attitude of obeying God rather than man.

There is a beautiful illustration of this kind of attitude in the book of Acts. When Peter and John were walking into the temple one day, they stopped and, through the power of God, healed a man who had been lame for forty years. All the commotion caused by this incident troubled the Council of the temple so much that they put Peter and John in jail and "commanded them not to speak or teach at all in the name of Jesus. But Peter and John answered and said to them, 'Whether it is right in the sight of God to give heed to you rather than to God, you be the judge; for we cannot stop speaking what we have seen and heard!' " (Acts 4:18-20). What a spirit of meekness and confidence! They were then released from jail, as it was obvious to all that a genuine miracle had taken place.

A couple of days later Peter and John were put in jail again for disobeying the Council's command. "But an angel of the Lord during the night opened the gates of the prison, and, taking them out, he said, 'Go your way, stand and speak to the people in the temple the whole message of this Life' " (Acts 5:19-20). The next morning the Council had them brought up again. The high priest questioned them, saying: "We gave you strict orders not to continue teaching in this name, and behold, you have filled Jerusalem with your teaching.' . . . But Peter and the apostles answered and said, 'We must obey God rather than men' " (Acts 5:28-29). And God assisted them in their disobedience by engineering a jail break. The disciples were told a third time by the Council not to speak in the name of Jesus and then were released again. "And every day, in the temple and from house to house, they kept right on teaching and preaching Jesus as the Christ" (Acts 5:42).

A time to disobey? Certainly! The early church was guilty of civil disobedience throughout the first two centuries under Rome. They didn't disobey because they believed in Jesus, but because they did not view the Roman Emperor as God.

And there are similar situations today. What about the Jewish child who receives Christ in high school or college and then receives a directive from his parents to put a halt to this Christianity business? When he has taken the time to pursue the suggested process and still finds no alternatives, he must disobey!

This brings us to the final and most painful suggestion. (6) *Be willing to suffer the consequences*. The disciples were willing to go to jail and suffer the consequences of their decision. The Jewish child must be willing to suffer the consequences of his decision. It may be the silent treatment, removal from his home, a mock funeral, or even physical abuse. Obeying God and disobeying man is not always easy, The consequences may be devastating!

There is a time to obey and a time to disobey. May God give us the wisdom to know what time it is and the boldness to act accordingly!

FOOTNOTES

Chapter 11

1. J. Grant Howard, Jr., *Knowing God's Will and Doing It!* (Grand Rapids, MI: Zondervan Pub. House, 1976), pp. 27-28.

Twelve

AREN'T WE JUST TALKING TO OURSELVES?

"Have you heard of the four spiritual laws? "Have you heard of the five keys to happiness?" "Well, how about the ABC's to the abundant life?" In a day when evangelistic methods and training packages range from the "Four Laws" to the "Five Keys" to the "ABC's" to the "Three Steps and a Hop," we must stop long enough to ask ourselves *who in the world is listening?* Are we being effective with all of our talking and packaging and marketing of methods and materials, or *are we just talking to ourselves?* The constitution guarantees free speech, but it does not guarantee that people will listen. For the most part we do not need more methods, but an expanded understanding of what evangelism is all about.

As the biblical concept and practice of evangelism is examined, several significant principles emerge. *When these principles are followed, the non-believer hears the gospel in the context of real life needs, and there is adequate time for sufficient interaction and reflection before he receives it.* It is in this context that the gospel will most likely produce confident, healthy, fruit-bearing believers through its proclamation. When these principles are violated, those who need to hear the gospel are hearing, at best, a poor caricature of it.

The ones who receive the good news through inadequate means are often weak, plagued with doubts, and shallow in their growth. The ones who reject the gospel when it is presented through inadequate means have not been exposed to the truth as it relates to them. The result is that we're often just talking to ourselves. (It is important to note that God does prepare the hearts of some people to receive his message the first time they hear it.)

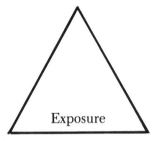

The Principle of Exposure

If we create evangelistic radio and TV programs and air them only on Christian radio and TV stations, *aren't we just talking to ourselves?* If we write evangelistic books or articles and publish them only in the Christian market, *aren't we just talking to ourselves?* If we present evangelistic messages only inside the church building or relate only to Christians while isolating ourselves from non-believers, *aren't we just talking to ourselves?*

The principles of the Bible relate to life as it is and to people where they are. Why not attempt to expose people to the gospel through the secular media—radio, TV, books, etc.? Why not attempt to expose people to the gospel outside the church buildings—in civic clubs, P.T.A., university and high school classrooms, etc.?

I have had good experiences in the last few years speaking to non-believer groups. As a matter of fact, this last year I have started speaking to the secular audience almost exclusively. It's the most incredible experience to see such an audience consume the biblical principles for a maximum life. One evening I spoke to the fathers of an elementary P.T.A. on "Maximum Parenthood." I gave them principles from the Bible on a game-plan for parenting but didn't tell them where they came from until the end. I said, "Do you know where I got those insights and principles? I read a good book on the subject—the Bible!" They were amazed. I was smothered with questions afterward from people wanting to know more. The next week I spoke to the mothers at the same school. They normally had approximately 50 women present. This time there were 250 women waiting to hear the biblical game-plan for parenting! People are hungry for answers. They really aren't concerned about where they come from as long as they work.

Aside from such special opportunities for one who speaks and writes, there are a multitude of everyday opportunities to expose people right where you are. Thousands of eager "evangelists" are stepping over their neighbors and fellow-workers at the office (a natural setting) in an attempt to reach the world for Christ somewhere else (an unnatural setting). Most believers are forced into unnatural evangelism (talking to strangers) because they don't have good friendship relationships with non-believers.

Many believers are so isolated that they don't even know an unbeliever, except on a superficial basis. When this is the case, *aren't we just talking to ourselves?* Others, who do have relationships with non-believers, feel so pressured to share the gospel, immediately and as frequently as possible, that they reflect a "holier-than-thou" attitude and don't relate to them as real human beings. This makes it impossible for the non-believer to observe true Christianity in its real-life context. However, even with the best possible exposure you still won't have effective evangelism. What you say and how you say it is extremely important.

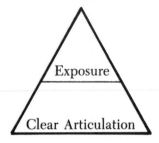

The Principle of Clear Articulation

If we present the gospel in our own cultural, churchy terms, so that we're actually speaking another language, *aren't we just talking to ourselves?* When a missionary prepares to go to a foreign country, he learns about its culture and studies its language. Otherwise, he couldn't relate to the people or talk to them about the gospel. In many cases we speak to the non-believer in a language foreign to him. Phrases and terms that he can't possibly understand are quoted to him with little or no explanation, as though he were familiar with them. "Receiving Christ," "guilt," "saved," "abundant life," "born again," and many other terms may be absolutely meaningless to the average twentieth century person. Jesus recognized that each individual has a different framework of knowledge, and He articulated the gospel accordingly.

If we use propagandizing methods which produce temporary decisions, *aren't we just talking to ourselves?* Propaganda is moving people to action without proper reflection. (Persuasion is moving people to action with proper reflection.) The salesman's method of closing a sale has permeated evangelism to the point that "closing the deal" is equated with evangelism. If a person is unsure of what he is doing or is not quite ready to make a decision and the "closer" is used prematurely, the evangelistic encounter borders on pure propaganda. When this is the case there are two possible results: a person may either profess a relationship with God without actually possessing it, or he may possess a relationship with God but be plagued by serious questions and doubts.

Every believer should be trained to be able to lead someone to accept Christ's payment for his or her sin (the "closer") when the opportunity arises, but to equate this act with evangelism is a devastating mistake. You will be hard-pressed to find anyone in the Bible praying with someone else to receive Christ as personal Savior. That is not evangelism. Evangelism is planting the seed and throwing a little water on it, counting on God to cause the increase (I Corinthians 3:4-9). It's making people think about their despair and their need for a Savior. It's making the issues clear. It's relating the gospel to their particular needs.

For some reason we feel we must constantly drop the answer (the gospel) on people and attempt to close the deal every opportunity we have. Consequently, we're always on the attack and put our friends on the defensive. They're just waiting for our pitch.

In making the transition from speaking primarily to Christian audiences to my present emphasis on secular groups, I have learned two very important lessons about communicating to the non-believer. The first is that you should strive to be the best at what you do. If you are a communicator, be the best! If you are a lawyer, be the best! If you are an artist or a musician, be the best! If you are a parent, be the best! By this you will clearly articulate that your approach to life is meaningful and beautiful.

The second lesson is to be satisfied to plant the seed and throw a little water on it. Don't feel compelled to close the deal. If I were to try to close the deal in my secular seminars, I would shut the door to speaking opportunities before thousands of hungry non-believers. I don't close any deals or have people pray with me for salvation, but I am diligently planting the seed of the good news of Jesus Christ.

An M.D. at my last seminar put it beautifully when he said: "I see what you are doing. You are helping people in the area of marriage in a significant way and then you're introducing the idea of a relationship with God at the appropriate time. Most of these people have rejected this God business. I've previously rejected it, but you made it seem so logical and true to life. You have certainly made me think!" That man got the point. Through being the best I can be in communicating marital and family principles and at the same time planting the seed, I am seeing many people receive Jesus Christ. (Many more than when I always felt compelled to use the "closer.") The reason for this increase in effectiveness is that I'm exposing more non-believers, clearly articulating the gospel as I plant the seed, and trusting God to close the deal. It works so much better that way! When God closes the deal, it lasts forever. When I close the deal, it has a built-in fizzle.

Yet if you have the best possible exposure and articulate clearly, but do not know *when* to speak, you still don't have effective evangelism

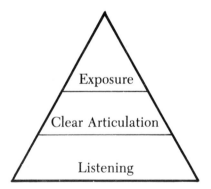

The Principle of Listening

If we say Christ is the answer, but we rarely grapple with the honest questions people are asking, *aren't we just talking to ourselves?* The non-believer's logical response to the believer's urgent and aggressive "Christ is the answer!" is "To what?" What is the question to which Christ is the answer? Each person is wrestling with a different question. Everyone is operating from a different area of need—someone from lack of security, another from lack of identity, or from unanswered intellectual questions, or marriage and family problems, or financial crises, or even from the lack of the basic necessities. Whatever a person's basic area of need is, that is the very area where the believer has the opportunity to demonstrate how Christ is the ultimate answer. A hungry non-believer cannot hear the gospel until he is given food to eat. A person craving to be loved cannot hear the gospel until genuine love is felt.

Any other approach borders on pharisaical hypocrisy. By it we are saying, "I'll tell about the gospel, but I don't care enough to feed you. I don't have time to demonstrate love to you." In other words, "I'm interested in another 'closer,' another decision, another notch on my spiritual gun handle, but I don't really have time for you and your needs." What a tragic attitude! It's so easy while talking to a non-believer to shake our heads mechanically, as if to say, "Yes, yes, I hear you," and then to pounce on him as soon as he stops to breathe and dump the gospel on him. We're not really listening.

Open Doors

In his letter to the Colossians Paul makes an interesting prayer request that reveals his strategy for evangelism: "Praying at the same time for us as well, *that God may open up to us a door for the word, so that we may speak forth the mystery of Christ,* for which I have also been imprisoned; in order *that I may make it clear in the way I ought to speak. Conduct yourselves with wisdom toward outsiders, making the most of your time.* Let your speech always be with grace, seasoned, as it were, with salt, *so that you may know how you should respond to each person*" (Colossians 4:3-6). Notice that it's God who opens up the door for the Word. We're not to push doors open, but to pray diligently and search for the doors that God has opened.

What is an "open door"? If you find yourself seated next to someone on the plane, is that an open door? Not necessarily. What about the checkout clerk at the grocery store, or your next door neighbor? Not necessarily. Any of these may or may not be an open door. The key element seems to be an openness within the person, created by the convicting work of the Holy Spirit. That openness might simply take the form of a warm response to you as a person. More likely it could be a need that is opened up to you with which you can empathize and to which you may be able to relate Christ. We must listen and speak carefully, "so that you may know how you should respond to each person."

Within the last two months I have observed seven men enter into a personal relationship with the Lord. Each one of them came to see me because of some personal or marital problem. Each of them made it clear that he did not want anything to do with religion. I assured him that I didn't either. In each case I helped the person with his problems and planted the seed of the good news at the same time. Unless I had first related to his immediate needs and problems, a presentation of the gospel would have been grossly out of place, but in its proper place (the open door) he understood it and received it. Why? Because God the Holy Spirit brought him to that point. My presence during the actual "closing" was purely incidental. I plant and water, but God closes the deal.

Whether you are relating to an individual or with a group of people, effective communication requires a careful analysis and knowledge of those you are relating with. The best way to achieve this and to be aware of any open door is to spend time together in meaningful activities. On the foundation of shared experiences the relationship can continue to build and more and more effective communication can take place. My wife and I are enjoying our relationship with our Jewish neighbors across the street. We're enjoying and listening and being involved in their lives. We are having fun with them. Doors have been opened by God. We have planted the seed and watered, but we remain real people with them—sharing in the joys and sorrows of life.

Be careful to avoid the two ineffective extremes here. *One is to articulate the gospel without any open door.* This extreme is offensive in an active sort of way. *The other extreme is to have an open door without any articulation of the gospel.* This is offensive in a passive sense. Both extremes are an obstacle to the Spirit's work.

However, even if there is the best possible exposure, clear articulation, and a sensitivity for listening, this is still not enough to produce effective evangelism. There is one final principle which serves as the foundation for the other three.

Exposure

Clear Articulation

Listening

Lifestyle

The Principle of Lifestyle

If we take the Christian lifestyle for granted and lay heavier emphasis on training in what to say and how to say it, *aren't we just talking to ourselves?* The children's chorus, "What you are speaks so loud that the world can't hear what you say," is quite profound. No matter how effectively we expose, how eloquently we speak, or how well we listen, unless our lifestyle backs up what we say our communication is nullified.

What is our lifestyle to be? As we have seen in Part One, Jesus describes it in two dimensions—salt and light! Salt refers primarily to who you are—your quality of life before God—the vertical relationship. Light refers primarily to what you do—your quality of life before people—the horizontal relationship. Salt and light, the vertical and the horizontal dimensions that must be seen by the non-believer. We are to let our light shine forth, not that the world may *hear what we say*, but that they may *see our good works*—our lifestyle. This reiterates the necessity of having a good relationship with non-believers, so that they may truly see our lifestyle. *Salt must touch the meat in order to be an effective preservative. Light must touch the darkness in order to be an effective projection.*

The best illustration of the importance of lifestyle to the communication of the gospel is found in I Thessalonians 2. Paul says the reason the Thessalonians received the gospel was because of his lifestyle *in their midst*—his character before God (salt) and his compassion for them as people (light).

Effective evangelism occurs when the non-believer hears the gospel in the context of real-life needs has adequate opportunity for clear observation of the quality of lifestyle it produces and takes the time for proper reflection before making a decision. Although there are exceptions, this seems to be the most biblical, effective, and natural strategy for evangelism.

Evangelism? Aren't we just talking to ourselves? *We're judging the world and talking to ourselves when we should be judging ourselves and talking to the world.*

Part Four

PROCESS—HOW IS THE ULTIMATE LIFESTYLE LIVED?

Thirteen

PEOPLE WHO NEED PEOPLE

It was turning out to be a terribly frustrating day of golf for old George. He just kept missing the ball and digging up a lot of dirt. It was on the ninth hole that he took a stroke, missed the ball and disrupted a large ant hill nearby. He got set, took another swing and missed again, wiping out another large section of the ant hill. Ants were flying everywhere, but the ball hadn't moved. Observing the seriousness of their situation, one ant turned and said to another, "If we don't get on the ball, we're going to be killed!" That could be taken as a challenge to many Christians as well.

Even if we have brought into balance our perspective ("What is the Christian lifestyle?"), our participation ("Who lives it?"), and our position ("Where is it lived?"), we cannot pull it all together without a proper understanding of the process ("How is it lived?").

The Predicament

As I travel in this country and internationally, I sense that there is a predicament of despair among believers. It manifests itself in a number of different forms. Problems related to self-image are among the most prevalent. One young man came into my office week after week. He was filled with depression and just couldn't snap out of it. Our counseling sessions seemed effective and he was temporarily helped by them, but as soon as he reached the parking lot his despair returned.

Other forms of the predicament involve addiction (drug, alcohol, sex, etc.). I remember a casual friend who had everything a man could want in life, but he was being devoured by his problem of alcoholism. He just couldn't seem to break his destructive habit. There was a woman who was sexually addicted. She found herself in affair after affair with married men, and although she would cry in despair and make strong resolutions to quit, within a week she was back in the sack with another man.

Sometimes the predicament involves Satan's counterfeit teachings. They seem to surround us on every side, bouncing the believers around like a ping-pong ball. The predicament may also be reflected in stunted spiritual growth. The desires and pressures of the world system weigh many believers down to a nod-to-God lifestyle. In other cases the hassles of everyday living are so stressful that many believers put their spiritual life on automatic pilot, while under the surface they harbor gnawing questions and doubts. Is God really in my life?

The predicament of despair lingers like a dark cloud over many lives. It all seems to boil down to one common denominator—the inability to experience God, His presence and His power. "God, if I could just touch You, then I would clean up my act and live for You." If I could only know for sure that You are there!" "God, I would go through anything if I could just experience Your power one time!"

The Problem

What is the problem? Why can't we rise out of our predicaments of despair? Why do we often feel that we have never experienced God's presence and power, or at least are not experiencing it now? There are certainly many ways of answering these questions. We've tried to cover all the bases in the earlier parts of this book, but there is one problem that is usually overlooked! *Christians are trying to live the Christian lifestyle all alone.* Many are looking upward and crying out to God for an answer to their dilemma while isolating themselves from vital relationships around them. *God doesn't work in a vacuum, He works through His Word and through His people.*

The two most basic institutions created by God illustrate this very clearly—the home and the church. God's creation of the first home is recorded in Genesis 1 and 2. He created the earth and said, "This is good!" He created the plants and said, "These are good!" He created the animals and said, "These are good!" Then God created Adam and said, "This is *not* good!" No doubt Adam responded, "Who, me?" Imagine the shock! He had a good job, a good employer and nice retirement benefits. He had it made. He even had something you and I can't have—a perfect relationship with God. Yet in spite of that, God clearly declared the situation "not good." "It is not good for the man to be alone" (Genesis 2:18). Adam was incomplete and he needed someone to complete him. The Lord knew the solution, "I will make him a helper suitable for him." I can imagine Adam's response to this: "But God, can't you meet my needs of being alone through our vertical relationship?" Yes, the Lord could have met his needs vertically, but that's not what He chose to do. God chose to meet his needs horizontally—through creating a mate for him.

God did a strange thing with Adam. He brought all the animals He had created to Adam so that he could examine and name them and look among them for a helpmate. Adam didn't know any better. He had never seen a woman before. Why did God have Adam name the animals before giving him a wife? Primarily, He wanted to demonstrate to him the nature of his incompleteness, and also to give him a sense of appreciation for the woman He was about to create for him. Through the naming of the animals, the Lord wanted Adam to realize that nothing else in the creation would be able to meet his needs of aloneness. The Lord created the only one who could meet his needs for completion—woman. When Adam saw Eve for the first time, he responded ecstatically: "This is now bone of my bones, and flesh of my flesh; she shall be called Woman, because she was taken out of man" (Genesis 2:23). Now that hardly sounds like ecstasy. The problem is in the translation of the phrase "this is now." Have you ever gone to a football game and at an exciting moment stood up and screamed, "This is now!"? I hope not! The Hebrew "this is now" is not a calm expression of conversation. It's an exclamation having the force of, "Wow! Wrap it up! I'll take it!" In front of God and all the animals, Adam went berserk. He was ecstatic.

Now why didn't Adam react against his mate's weaknesses as many do? She certainly had a few. She even proved it in the next chapter! His response might have been, "Lord, while you're creating—she's a little chunky. Could You slim her down?" She's too tall!" "Lord, she talks too much!" I think the reason Adam didn't react in this way was because he realized Eve was a gift from God to bring him perfect completeness. Therefore, to reject Eve in any way was to reject God Himself and His design. So Adam *received* (not merely accepted) Eve as his completer. *God doesn't work in a vacuum, He works through His Word and through His people*.

The second institution created by God is the church—the body of believers. This is another good illustration of how God works through people. A startling assumption is made in Ephesians 4:11-16, that spiritual growth occurs when all individual parts work properly together. In other words, we desperately need one another in order to grow spiritually. You won't grow alone, but you will in relationship with other members of the body. This relationship is more than being a member of the church. It involves functioning and interacting together toward the building up of one another.

The Provision

God never intended that we should live the Christian life alone, but rather in relationship. He has provided for our needs and the solutions to our problems through other members of the body. This body concept permeates the New Testament. Most of the epistles were written to a body of believers. That's why Paul keeps saying "you all." He wasn't a southerner. He was speaking in the plural. Our problem is that for the most part we have applied his teachings in the singular.

I used to have a great message on Colossians 3:16. "Let the word of Christ dwell within you richly." I really got a lot of mileage out of this verse in teaching the importance of meditation (dwelling within you). Then I realized that the "you" is not singular, but plural. It's not "dwell within you," but "dwell among you." So Paul is not speaking of meditation, but of allowing the Word of Christ to dwell among us when we meet and interact together. The rest of the verse explains it perfectly: ". . . with all wisdom teaching and admonishing one another with psalms and hymns and spiritual songs, singing with thankfulness in your hearts to God" (Colossians 3:16). As each member participates by sharing a passage of Scripture, an insight from Scripture or a song, God dwells among us. That's dynamite!

Another illustration of how God uses other people to meet our needs is found in II Corinthians 7:5-7. Paul says, "For even when we came into Macedonia our flesh had no rest, but we were afflicted on every side; conflicts without, fears within. But God, who comforts the depressed, comforted us . . ." That makes it sound as if God just zapped him with comfort when He needed it. Why doesn't God do that for me? Let's read on: "But God, who comforts the depressed, *comforted us by the coming of Titus*; and not only by his coming, but also by the comfort with which he was comforted in you, as he reported to us your longing, your mourning, your zeal for me;

so that I rejoiced even more." Paul is saying something very profound, but it's often skipped over. *"God touched me through Titus and God touched Titus through the Corinthians."*

There are practical illustrations of this same truth all around you. If you would draw a "life-line," tracing it horizontally across the page, and make it turn up during growth times and down during non-growth times, you'd find that your growth patterns nearly always occur in significant relationships with other members of the body of Christ. That's why we are exhorted to "weep with those who weep and rejoice with those who rejoice," to bear one another's burdens and to love one another. Paul sums it up well in Galatians 5:25: "If we live by that which is spirit [the new nature], let us also walk [keep in step with others] by that which is spirit" (partial paraphrase). Why? *Because God doesn't work in a vacuum, He works through His Word and through His people.*

Two very essential questions of application must be faced in light of God's pattern of working through people. The first is: *Will you commit yourself to minister to every member of the body?* It's always easier to assist or minister to those who are lovable. The tendency is to send the "uglies" down the street to someone else. The first question is a real soul-searcher, but the second one is a killer: *Will you allow each member of the body to minister to you?* This is the tough one for me.

In the fall of 1973, my mother entered the hospital in Cincinnati, Ohio, eaten up with cancer. I was in Dallas teaching graduate school and carrying a heavy counseling load. As I was an only child and my dad was already dead, I desperately wanted to be with her. During the two months it took me to prepare to leave Dallas, my men's Bible study group flew me to Cincinnati every three days. I'd catch the 6:30 A.M. flight out and return to Dallas that same night at 1:30 A.M. Finally I moved with my family up to Cincinnati into a one bedroom apartment across from the hospital. We were with Mom night and day for nearly two months, watching her transition from a beautiful, vibrant woman to a very weak, lifeless body.

While we were watching her die, I was being harassed by a person in Dallas threatening to sue me. He called and called, ranting and raving and cursing me out. The moment Mom died I was listening to that barrage of garbage on the other end of the phone. We were under a great deal of pressure. Needless to say, the funeral was not a time of mourning, but of relief. My mourning had been going on for almost a year, ever since I was first told of my mother's condition. We had always enjoyed such a close relationship, but now there would be no more calls, no more newsy letters, no more stops through Cincinnati to go home, no more grandmother for my little ones, no more Mom.

Three weeks after the funeral I was on the road again speaking in conferences. But there was something wrong when I got up to speak. *I didn't care about people anymore.* That scared me. I realized that the shock of my mother's death had drained me totally. I cancelled almost every speaking engagement I had for the spring, and through the next five months my wife and I talked and cried to each other and to God about my problem.

I kept one speaking engagement in June at a downtown church in Los Angeles. I was to speak at their annual family conference—three services on Sunday and meetings the following four evenings. At the first Sunday service I felt pretty good, but still it wasn't the same. After the service, I stood in the front as usual waiting for people to come and greet me. No one came at first, except one little old man. He wore a dark green sport coat and a dirty pair of black slacks which didn't match. His yellowed white shirt had a button missing at the top, and his extremely thin plain tie looked like it came out of the 50's. This man talked to me about everything under the sun for an hour! Other people would try to say something, but he just increased his volume. I couldn't believe it.

When I returned to my hotel room, I prayed that little old man wouldn't make it to the afternoon service. But when I stood up to speak in the afternoon service, I saw that he was sitting in his same seat right in the front row. I decided to try to fake him out at the end of my message. When the service was over I took two steps to the right, and he went with the fake. Just at that moment I pivoted and headed to the other side of the platform. I thought by the time he had recovered from that fantastic fake I would be swarmed over by all the "lovely" people wanting to talk to me. Well, it didn't happen. He went for the fake alright, but the lovely people didn't swarm—nobody swarmed. So the little old man trotted over from the other end of the platform and began talking away just as he had at the morning service.

When I stood up to speak at the evening service I felt great. The little old man's seat in the front row was empty. Then right at the close of my introduction I saw him coming down the aisle. This was too much! At the end of the message I decided to stay up on the platform, surely he would never be bold enough to walk up here to talk with me. *Strike three!* I was wrong again. He walked up the steps and came over to me—but this time it was all different! He had tears streaming down his face, and he said, "It must be a real privilege to run around the country and speak to people about the Lord Jesus." At that moment God touched me. It was as though God performed a psychological healing through this man I had so diligently resisted. I cared about people again as I had before—I really cared! I had been crying out to God for months to touch me and restore my compassion, but at the same time I was resisting and rejecting His messenger to me.

God doesn't work in a vacuum, but through His Word and through His people. Possibly you have some struggles and problems for which you are seeking the healing hand of God. Perhaps the answer to your needs is to be found within another part of the body. Every part of the body needs you and you need every part of the body for maximum spiritual growth. *God doesn't work in a vacuum.*

Fourteen

"CRIMINAL" EVIDENCE: THE SUPERNATURAL REVELATION!

Agnosticism . . . mysticism . . . atheism . . . pantheism . . . humanism . . . Zen Buddhism . . . existentialism. . . . As the labels of life continue to flow ad nauseum, people are swinging from one side of the pendulum to the other. The result is that many are suffering from "ism-itis." "Ism-itis" is a sort of motion sickness caused from swinging on the pendulum or watching others swing. Because of the resulting dizziness, very few people have stopped long enough to consider the overwhelming evidence that the personal God of the universe has revealed Himself by written (Bible) and human (Jesus of Nazareth) means and desires a relationship with people.

I'm not talking about religion. Religion destroys people. Jesus told the religious leaders of His day that they were "snakes" and "painted tombstones." He was down on religion, and so am I. When I wanted to obtain my "ticket to heaven," I was told by religion that there were fifteen things I couldn't do. As I looked over the list, I was immediately depressed. Those were my goals in life! Then I was told there were four things I could do—that I must do: 1) go to church on Sunday morning, 2) go to church on Sunday evening, 3) go to church on Wednesday evening, and 4) pray before every meal. It all spelled out a four letter word to me—BORE! Then I ran into a group that said all I had to do to get my ticket was to let them dunk me in their tank. (This comes in various forms: sprinkling, squirting, drowning, dry-cleaning, etc.) The only thing I gained from that experience was a wet body. No, I'm not talking about religion. Because it blindly accepts a certain system of do's and don'ts and ignores more basic issues, religion makes life miserable. It is comparable to a sedative given to a dying person. It may make them feel better, but they are still dying.

The supernatural factor is also not a blind or mystical leap in the dark whereby one hopes to find meaning to life. It's based on evidence and logic. It's not a nebulous, evasive or untouchable factor. It's a body of solid facts upon which we can hang our faith, clearly laid out so that we can know and understand them.

To many people evidence means absolutely nothing. Clark Pinnock relates an illustration of this:

> "Once upon a time there was a man who thought he was dead. His concerned wife and friends sent him to the friendly neighborhood psychiatrist. The psychiatrist determined to cure him by convincing him of one fact that contradicted his belief that he was dead. The psychiatrist decided to use the simple truth that dead men do not bleed. He put his patient to work reading medical texts, observing autopsies, etc. After weeks of effort, the patient finally said, 'All right, all right! You've convinced me. Dead men do not bleed.' Whereupon the psychiatrist stuck him in the arm with a needle, and the blood flowed. The man looked down with a contorted, ashen face and cried: 'Good Lord! Dead men bleed after all!'"[1]

If however, you are willing to acknowledge the available evidence, examine it honestly and make a reasoned evaluation, we can begin to think through the supernatural factor. I challenge you to face these facts openly.

The Supernatural Revelation

We began this book by analyzing the question, "If Christianity were a crime, would there be enough evidence to convict you?" Now I'd like to apply the same metaphor in a little different way, by asking, "If Christianity were a crime, what kind of 'criminal evidence' would persuade a person that it is worthy of 'conviction' as 'guilty' of being true?"

Unity

The first piece of "criminal" evidence I would like to consider is whether the Bible, comprised of the Old Testament and the New Testament, is a revelation from God. In order for you to think this through, I'd like to offer you just a few reasons why I believe it is.

The first reason I believe the Bible is a supernatural revelation from God is that it has incredible unity. It was written over a period of fifteen hundred years, by forty different writers, in three different languages, and on three different continents. A lot of people think that some group back in Jerusalem got together—the First Bapterian Church or the Episcolics—and decided to write a bunch of books. Then year after year they submitted them to the University of Jerusalem, who at last one day put them to press and called them the Bible. That's not true. It was written over many centuries, and yet with unbelievable unity. You can read modern books on different subjects, even from one university, from one school of thought, and you will find vast differences. There may be people working on the same committee, trying to come up with some sort of book, and they'll disagree even on what chapters should be included. So when you find a book written over a long period of time, in a number of languages, by people with wide cultural differences, and still see unity—you have something you had better look into.

You will see the Old Testament, bursting and screaming out that there is a Messiah coming, a Messiah who is needed because we are wicked people who need to have our sin paid for. He's coming—He's coming. You will see the New Testament, revealing a Messiah who has come to pay for our sin. He's come—He's come. You see the tying of the two together, and it's absolutely beautiful. The unity.

Accuracy

The second reason why I believe that the Bible is a revelation from God is its accuracy. I divide this subject into two parts: the archaeological accuracy and the historical accuracy. I'm just going to give you a taste of each of these and try to highlight some of the evidence they offer.

The first is the Bible's archaeological accuracy. I have enjoyed reading a lot of archaeology over the years, and especially the works of Dr. Albright, professor emeritus at Johns Hopkins University. Dr. Albright was a brilliant scholar in his field, but when he moved out of archaeology into prophecy he was horrible. He made statements such as "We can't find the Hittites!" (The Hittites were a large, much talked about group of people in the Old Testament.) Albright and his companions said, "Well, where are they? This just proves once again that the Bible is inaccurate." Then some archaeologist would come along and say, "Guess what, I was digging a hole over there in the Middle East and I found the Hittites!" The most embarassing moment in the life of an archaeologist turned prophet, is when someone digs up what he said didn't exist. (By the way, Albright prophesied in 1948 that the Jews would not go back into their land and become a state.) If he opened his mouth to prophesy, you were sure to win if you chose the opposite opinion. Nevertheless, Albright was a great archaeologist, and after a life of study and excavation in the Middle East he concluded, "There can be no doubt that archaeology has confirmed the substantial historicity of Old Testament tradition.[2]

Albright's conclusion is supported by that of Sir Frederic Kenyon, the former director of the British Museum,

> "It is therefore legitimate to say that, in respect of that part of the Old Testament against which the disintegrating criticism of the last half of the nineteenth century was chiefly directed, the evidence of archaeology has been to reestablish its authority and likewise to augment its value by rendering it more intelligible through a fuller knowledge of its background and setting. Archaeology has not yet said its last word, but the results already achieved confirm what faith would suggest—that the Bible can do nothing but gain from an increase in knowledge."[3]

These experts attest to the Bible's archaeological accuracy.

Then there is the matter of its historical accuracy. There was a man by the name of Sir William Ramsay who set out to prove the Bible false by using its historical events and then proving them wrong, especially in the book of Acts. He decided he was going to go everywhere and do everything that Luke recorded about himself, Paul and the others in the book of Acts, and thereby show that it couldn't be done. For example, taking a boat from one point to another in a certain period of time. He took the same kind of boat that they must have had, left from the same place and journeyed to the same place, trying to see if they could have made it in the recorded period of time. When he got through with his study, he not only accepted Jesus Christ as His Savior, but he made the statement that Luke was probably the most accurate historian of his time.

> "Luke is a historian of the first rank; not merely are his statements of fact trustworthy; he is possessed of the true historic sense; he fixed his mind on the idea and plan that rules in the evolution of history, and proportions the scale of his treatment to the importance of each incident. . . . In short, this author should be placed along with the very greatest of historians."[4]

He was overwhelmed with the Bible's historical accuracy.

Now this accuracy does not prove that the Bible is supernatural, but it does indicate that if it is accurate in the details—in the things that don't matter a whole lot—it is more likely to be accurate in the things that do matter a whole lot.

I think it is also important to point out how the biblical documents compare with other ancient documents. Now most ancient documents aren't the type of reading one would typically pick up for an evening's enjoyment. But then again, maybe some of you would. One night I was speaking on this and commented, "Now there's Tacitus, whom some of you probably read last night" (just joking, and everyone laughed). One lady in the front said, "I did, I did!" She was an exception, I'm sure. Tacitus was a Roman historian of the late first and early second centuries. One thousand years later, there were twenty copies of what he wrote. The original had been lost—only twenty copies existed. Caesar's *Gallic Wars*, have the same kind of spread. Only eight copies exist today. Thucydides, a Greek writer often cited, is represented by five or six documents after a period of thirteen hundred years.

Now no one is getting really upset about the accuracy of what these writers said. No one is very interested in it, and no one questions it. Kenyon comments, "Scholars are satisfied that they possess substantially the true text of the principal Greek and Roman writers whose works have come down to us, of Sophocles, of Thucydides, of Cicero, of Virgil; yet our knowledge of their writings depends on a mere handful of manuscripts, whereas the manuscripts of the New Testament are counted by hundreds, and even thousands."[5]

Now when we bring the Bible into focus here, and compare it with these other ancient documents, we find it is supported by the strongest evidence possible. Kenyon continues:

> "It cannot be too strongly asserted that in substance the text of the Bible is certain. Especially is this the case with the New Testament. The number of manuscripts of the New Testament, of early translations from it, and of quotations from it in the oldest writers of the Church, is so large that it is practically certain that the true reading of every doubtful passage is preserved in some one or other of these ancient

authorities. This can be said of no other ancient book in the world."[6]

There are thousands of manuscripts of portions of the Bible, some of them written within sixty, fifty, and even forty years of the event.

It's been interesting to watch how scholars keep moving the dates of the Gospels back. They used to say the Gospels were written about A.D. 110. Then they moved it to A.D. 100, A.D. 90, A.D. 80, A.D. 70, and they are still moving it back today. Through more and more historical discoveries, we are finding that the Gospels were written very close to the event. Harold J. Greenlee, professor of New Testament Greek at Oral Roberts University, states, "The earliest extant manuscripts of the New Testament were written much closer to the date of the original writing than is the case in almost any other piece of ancient literature."[7]

In the Old Testament we have a manuscript that is dated A.D. 900. Because that used to be the oldest manuscript of the Old Testament, many have speculated, "Well, if the Old Testament we have is dated A.D. 900, certainly a lot of inaccuracies must have developed in the hundreds of years before, a lot of bad copying and that kind of thing." This kind of speculation leads to some very interesting arguments. As a matter of fact, some Jewish scholars have said that Isaiah 53 (which prophesies that the Messiah will come and suffer for the sins of the world) was written by the Church. "There's no doubt about it, it had to be; it sounds too much like Jesus."

In Micah 5:2, it says that the Messiah will be born in Bethlehem. Liberal scholars have estimated that Micah was written around 250 B.C., but they are quick to make an exception for that one verse. They don't like that verse, because it talks about the Messiah being born in Bethlehem. That's supernatural! Therefore, it must have been inserted after the event.

Then the Dead Sea Scrolls were found. These Old Testament manuscripts are dated at approximately 150 B.C. All of these scrolls (and they are still being worked on) have proven to be 98.33% exactly the same as documents dated later.[8] "It is a matter of wonder that through something like a thousand years the text underwent so little alteration. As I said in my first article on the scroll, 'Herein lies its chief importance, supporting the fidelity of the Massoretic tradition.' "[9] There were very few inaccuracies, very few changes—it's amazing! Every book in the Old Testament is represented in the discovery of the Dead Sea Scrolls except the book of Esther.

Isaiah 53 is there, and if you can read the Hebrew, you can go to the Shrine of the Scroll in Jerusalem some day and say, "Yes, that's it, that's Isaiah 53, I saw it!" It was not written by the Church, but was in existence for at least two centuries before the Church was founded.

> "Of the 166 words in Isaiah 53, there are only seventeen letters in question. Ten of these letters are simply a matter of spelling, which does not affect the sense. Four more letters are minor stylistic changes, such as conjunctions. The remaining three letters comprise the word 'light,' which is added in verse 11, and does not affect the meaning greatly. . . . Thus, in one chapter of 166 words, there is only one word (three letters) in question after a thousand years of transmission—and this word does not significantly change the meaning of the passage."[10]

Micah 5:2 was there, too. All the things that had been thrown up as inaccuracies were there, a thousand years before the A.D. 900 manuscript.

I have a friend, his name is Arnold Fruchtenbaum. He's a Hebrew-Christian. Arnold's grandfather was the rabbi of the largest Hasiddic (very, very, very conservative) Jewish sect in the world, located in Siberia where he was born. His grandfather knew the Torah (the first five books of the Bible) so well that when a spike was driven through it, he could tell exactly which words it had touched on every page. That's an example of the standard of accuracy with which they copied and transferred the Word of God. They considered it the holy Word of God. They counted the words within a book to make sure they had the exact number, and so many words on each page. They were very, very careful, and they produced a very, very accurate copy of the original.

Prophecy

In my opinion, a lot of bad stuff has come out on prophecy, most of which isn't worth looking into. For instance, some have said that the red dragon in Revelation must mean China. Why is that? You can't reason from what you see around you and then decide what you want a verse to be talking about. When you are trying to find out what a verse in the Bible means, you have to study how it was used within its cultural setting. Some teachers of prophecy say that when Revelation speaks of people mounting up with wings as eagles and fleeing to the mountains it means that Israelis are going to be fleeing their land in United States airplanes (the eagle being a symbol for the U.S.A.). That's ridiculous! Such thinking has no controls. Whatever you think is there is there, and that's foolishness.

There are two things that I belive are very clear in prophecy—Christ's first coming and Christ's second coming. In discussing the first coming I will mention eight specific prophecies that are very simple, but very interesting. When Christ came on the scene, there were two concepts concerning the Messiah: one was that the Messiah was going to come and reign, the other that the Messiah was going to come and die. Now, if you were a Jew, sitting in captivity under the persecution and harassment of the Romans, which Messiah would you like to have come? It was not time for one to die, that's for sure! Although some were still holding to the two-Messiah concept at Christ's coming, there were many who believed just what the Old Testament prophesied. It said He was: 1) to be born in Bethlehem,[11] 2) to be preceded by a messenger,[12] 3) to enter Jerusalem on a donkey,[13] 4) to be betrayed by a friend,[14] 5) to be sold for thirty pieces of silver,[15] 6) This money was to be thrown down in God's house and given for a potters field,[16] 7) He did not retaliate against his accusers,[17] 8) His hands and feet were to be pierced,[18] and He would be crucified with thieves.[19]

Peter Stoner, in a book entitled *Science Speaks*, calculates that the possibility of a person fulfilling all eight of these would be one times ten to the seventeenth power. I'm not much of a mathematician, but I believe that's one with seventeen zeros following it, and those are high odds. Stoner made the analogy: take that many silver dollars, one times ten to the seventeenth power, lay them on the surface of Texas, and they will cover all of the state two feet deep; mark one of them, stir it up with the others, blindfold a man, and he must pick up the marked coin in his first try. One times ten to the seventeenth power. That's very difficult! Now if the number of prophecies were increased from eight to forty-eight (there are about sixty major ones in all), consider the possibility of one person fulfilling all of them. These prophecies don't deal with generalities—such as it will be a depressing day, the economy will have a bad time, there will be clouds this month. They are very specific. The possibility that all forty-eight of these would by chance be true of one man is one times ten to the 157th power. That's a lot of zeros![20]

One of the prophecies of Christ's first coming that I think is especially outstanding is Daniel 9:24-27. There it says that 483 years after the decree to rebuild Jerusalem and its walls (given in 445 B.C.) The Messiah, the Prince, will come. I believe that's why many people, as we see in the Gospels, were looking for the Messiah at that time, because it was around A.D. 30 that the Messiah, the Prince, was to come.[21] That's a pretty accurate prophecy written five hundred years before Jesus ever came on the scene.

The second coming is also very interesting. The Bible prophesies in what context the Messiah will come and what state the world is going to be in when He comes to set up His kingdom. In Leviticus 26, Deuteronomy 28 and Deuteronomy 30 we read that although Israel will be scattered throughout the world, she will return to her land and become a nation. The fulfillment of this occurred in 1949. It was also prophesied that she would take over the city of Jerusalem.

This didn't happen until 1967, in the Six Day War.

The third thing it says about Israel is that she will rebuild the temple before Jesus comes back to reign. On the sixth day of the Six Day War, when Israel was going in to take the city of Jerusalem, some scrolls were found at the edge of the city. These were called the "Temple Scrolls," and they were written up in *Time, Newsweek*, etc. The scrolls will be used as instructions to rebuild the Temple on its historic site.

As some of you know, this might present a little problem. You can't build a temple on that site until the little building presently there is moved off, and the little building presently on the site belongs to the Arabs. The Mosque of Omar (The Dome of the Rock) is the second most holy spot in the Islamic religion—the religion of the Arab world. One sure-fire way to get a few Arabs hot is to start knocking down that building! When Hildad, the Israeli Historian, was asked, "When are you going to build the temple?" he said, "Well, it will probably take us a generation, just as it did with David when he came back from the land." They replied, "But what about that temple over there, what about that mosque?" He smiled and answered, "Maybe there will be an earthquake, who knows?" Jews who take the Old Testament seriously are talking about the temple. They are even selling temple bonds, if you care to buy them, in L.A. or Miami.

There is also a prophecy in Ezekiel 1:38 which states that the King of the North (from the northernmost parts of Israel) will come and set up an alignment of powers with the nations immediately bordering Israel. If you take a line directly north from Israel, you come to the King of the North, which I believe is the Russian government. Whether they will be in the form they are now or not, I don't know. Neither do I know when all this will happen. I'm just trying to help set a possible context here. The Russian people did not go against Israel in an alignment of power with the Arab nations until 1967. They were trying to get Israel without going to war against her, so they armed the Arabs and took the side of the Arab people. It happened just as Ezekiel said it would.

It's also interesting to note that prophecy indicates that the economic center of the world will be moved to the Middle East. In Zechariah 5:5-11 it says that the *ephah*, a Hebrew term used for the commercial center, will be moved to Shinar. Shinar is a Middle East location, and this prophecy indicates that before the Messiah comes back the economic center, the commercial center of the world, will be in Shinar. Who would have thought a few years ago that this Middle East oil mess would so radically alter world economics right now, in this time, in our day? Things seem to be falling into place for the Messiah to come back. I don't think it's wise to talk about time, but I do think it's interesting to see that world events are occurring just as the Bible said they would.

The ecological problems we are facing today are also talked about in the Bible. A lot of people say, "Hey, wait a minute, you can't talk about wars and rumors of wars and famines and earthquakes as being a fulfillment of prophecy. There have always been wars and rumors of wars, there have always been famines, there have always been earthquakes!" That's true, but when Christ talks about these He speaks of them as birth pangs, and He says that there will be more and more of them, and they will be more intensive. It's like the intensity of pain a woman experiences while giving birth to a child. The birth pangs occur more frequently and become more intense until finally she gives birth. That's the image that Christ is trying to present. Unity, accuracy, prophecy— both of the first and second coming.

The fourth reason why I believe the Bible is a supernatural revelation from God is the claim to deity that Jesus made. he came saying this—"I am the God-Man." He said it in many ways. "If you've heard Me, you've heard God."[22] "If you've seen Me, you've seen God."[23] "If you know Me, you know God."[24] "If you've received Me, you've received God."[25] "If you've honored Me, you've honored God."[26] He was trying to get a point across—He was claiming to be equal to God. The chief priest walked up to Him in John 8 and said, "Are you the one who claims to be the Messiah, from the Old Testament?" And He said, "Yes, that's me." Many liberal scholars would say He didn't mean that. He meant something "deeper." It's like if I were to see an old acquaintance and say, "Bob, are you the same Bob Lowden that I remember attending a seminar a few years ago?" And he said, "Yeah, that's me." And I said, "Ah, really, you don't mean that, do you? You mean something 'deeper.'" No! He meant what he said—he's Bob Lowden. Jesus said exactly what He meant when He said He was the Messiah. "A man who can read the New Testament and not see that Christ claims to be more than a man, can look all over the sky at high noon on a cloudless day and not see the sun."[27]

C. S. Lewis, one of the greatest scholars of our century, argues it this way. The claim of Jesus that He was the God-Man is either true or false. If it's true, Jesus is the God-Man. If it's false, either He knew it was false, or he didn't know it was false. If He knew it was false—He really knew He wasn't the God-Man—but He was running around anyway saying, "I am the God-Man," what was He doing? Lying—He was an impostor! On the other hand, if He didn't know it was false—He thought He was the God-Man, but really wasn't—and He was running around saying, "I am the God-Man," what was He? He was nuts! That's it; those are the only alternatives we have. he was either lying, he was mentally unbalanced, or He actually was the God-Man.[28]

I AM THE GOD-MAN

Claims were False		Claims were True
		He is Lord
He knew they were false	He didn't know they were false	(Accept) (Reject)
(He was a liar)	(He was mentally unbalanced)	

Some people try to draw a line right down the center of this and say, "He was an outstanding teacher, the most exemplary person in the history of mankind. He would have made 'Who's Who in Jerusalem' if He had stuck around long enough. Too bad He died." But wait a minute, He didn't leave that alternative open to us. Either He was a liar, or He was mentally unbalanced, or He was the God-Man. Period.

Passing Jesus off as an outstanding teacher or a great example after hearing His claims would be synonymous to passing me off as a "great guy" after hearing me claim I was a poached egg. Imagine for a moment that I am not Tim Timmons, and I tell you, "Hey, I'm not Tim Timmons, I'm a poached egg." (Some of you may think, "Um, could be!") Now you would have to take me through the same kind of grid. I am either lying, mentally unbalanced, or I really am, I truly am, the first poached egg you have ever seen walk or talk. I guarantee though, after a very short time of my telling you that I am a poached egg, and you see that I really do believe I am a poached egg, you will not say, "You know, even though he claims to be a poached egg, he's a 'great guy.'" You don't do that with people like that. You get help for them!

Napoleon Bonaparte said, "I know men and I tell you that Jesus Christ is no mere man. Between Him and every other person in the world there is no possible term of comparison. Alexander, Caesar, Charlemagne and I have founded empires. But on what did we rest the creations of our genius? Upon force. Jesus Christ founded His empire upon love; and at this hour millions of men would die for Him."[29]

Jesus claimed to be the God-Man, and that claim is the best indication, the greatest proof, that there is something unusual about the Bible. He claimed that He was speaking from the Bible and that what He was saying was authoritatively coming from God. Many have claimed to be prophets or messengers from God. Jesus of Nazareth claimed to be God. He is the only man who has ever come along saying that He was the God-Man, and every one of us has to decide what to do with His claims.

The "criminal" evidence at this point is the discovery of a supernatural revelation from God to man. This supernatural revelation of God (both the written Word and the living

Word) lays a foundation for me to relate confidently to the supernatural God of the universe.

FOOTNOTES

Chapter 14

1. Clark H. Pinnock, *Set Forth Your Case* (Chicago: Moody, 1967), p. 124.
2. W. F. Albright, *Archaeology and the Religion of Israel* (Baltimore: Johns Hopkins, 1942), p. 176.
3. Sir Frederic Kenyon, *The Bible and Archaeology* (New York: Harper and Brothers, 1940), p. 279.
4. Sir W. M. Ramsay, *The Bearing of Recent Discovery on the Trustworthiness of the New Testament* (London: Hodder and Stoughton, 1915), p. 222.
5. Sir Frederic Kenyon, *Our Bible and the Ancient Manuscripts* (New York: Harper & Brothers, 1941), p. 23.
6. Ibid., p. 23.
7. J. Harold Greenlee, *Introduction to New Testament Textual Criticism* (Grand Rapids: Eerdmans, 1964), p. 15.
8. Norman L. Geisler and William E. Nix, *A general Introduction to the Bible* (Chicago: Moody, 1968), p. 365.
9. Ibid., p. 261.
10. Ibid., p. 263.
11. Prophecy: Micah 5:2, Fulfillment: Matthew 2:1.
12. Prophecy: Isaiah 40:3, Fulfillment: Matthew 3:1-2.
13. Prophecy: Zechariah 9:9, Fulfillment: Luke 19:35-37a.
14. Prophecy: Psalm 41:9, Fulfillment: Matthew 10:4.
15. Prophecy: Zechariah 11:12, Fulfillment: Matthew 26:15.
16. Prophecy: Zechariah 11:13b, Fulfillment: Matthew 27:5a.
17. Prophecy: Isaiah 53:7, Fulfillment: Matthew 27:12-19.
18. Prophecy: Psalm 22:16, Fulfillment: Luke 23:33.
19. Prophecy: Isaiah 53:12, Fulfillment: Matthew 27:38.
20. Peter W. Stoner, *Science Speaks* (Chicago: Moody, 1963), pp. 100-107.
21. Robert Anderson, *The Coming Prince* (Grand Rapids: Kregel), p. 127.

22. John 14:10.
23. John 14:9.
24. John 8:19.
25. Mark 9:37.
26. John 5:23.
27. Frank Mead (ed.), *The Encyclopedia of Religious Quotations* (Westwood: Fleming H. Revell, n.d.), p. 50.
28. C. S. Lewis, *Mere Christianity* (New York: MacMillan, 1943), p. 56.
29. Mead, op. cit., p. 56.

Fifteen

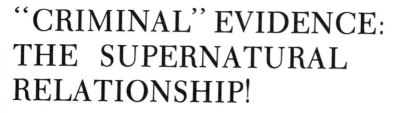

"CRIMINAL" EVIDENCE: THE SUPERNATURAL RELATIONSHIP!

It has been said, "The heart cannot delight in what the mind cannot accept." Because people continually ignore that principle, many have emotionally accepted or rejected Christianity without really understanding it. As Arnold Toynbee observed, "People have not rejected Christianity, but a poor caricature of it." The biblical revelation is not just another book of pious platitudes and religious rhetoric. It's a supernatural revelation that explains life as it is and people as they are. Built upon this crucial foundation is the reality of the supernatural relationship.

The Plan

According to the supernatural revelation, the original plan was for man to enjoy a relationship with God. It was through this relationship that man was to know and experience total fulfillment and full expression of himself as a human being. This relationship was intended to give man a reference point from which to enjoy life through relating properly to other people and to the entire creation.

The Problem

The plan was beautiful, but man botched it royally. As the bumper sticker says, "If you feel far from God, who moved?" Man finds himself separated from God and His plan because of his own self-centered rebellion.

Man has an optical problem—the big "I." "The world must revolve around me. God, you go your way, I'll go mine. Check with me when I'm seventy-one or seventy-two and we'll negotiate!" Man continues to wreck his life by rebelling against God's master plan of life, trying to run it on his own. Whether he experiences a personal crisis or an inner hollowness, his life is unsatisfying because he's not experiencing the maximum life for which he was created. The tragedy is that the effects of the wreckage of one's life are not limited to himself. It affects those around him as well. Without the supernatural, vertical relationship as a foundation, most horizontal relationships seem to disintegrate.

We have a desperate problem. We are separated from the God of the universe by our rebellion—our sin. It's like being separated by a great canyon that no one is able to cross on his own, even though we make many admirable attempts. Some try by living a good life. Some give to charities. Many become religious. Others try the intellectual route. Still no one is able to cross the canyon to the other side. It's humanly impossible!

Let's suppose that you and I are walking along the edge of a forty-foot canyon, and we want to get across to the other side. You suggest, "Let's jump!" I say, "O.K., but you go first!" So you back up about fifty yards and run like crazy toward the edge. As you spring from your side you push off with every ounce of strength you can muster. It's a noble jump—thirty-five feet, eleven inches. After I see you jump, I back up about ten yards and run toward the edge, giving it all I've got—ten feet, five and one-half inches. As you are soaring through the air in front of me, you glance back and think how much better you're doing than I. However, in a few seconds, we are both lying at the bottom of the canyon in critical condition. Why? People can't jump forty-foot canyons—they need a bridge.

The Payment

To put man's problem in another way, man is in debt to God. For our self-centered rebellion (our sin) God requires a payment. One of the most natural instincts of man is to try to pay for his own guilt. Man feels he must pay for what he does wrong and for his shortcomings. Everyone attempts to pay in different ways. Some pay by being down on themselves, even to the point of depression. Others pay by depriving themselves of something. An increasing number are attempting to make the ultimate payment by killing themselves, but none of these self-imposed payments really satisfies. The debt remains—man is guilty before God.

Counseling rooms are filled with people who are guilt ridden, seeking for a payment that will give them the confidence that the debt is paid. Professional counselors offer three possible payments. First is the transfer method: "Blame it on someone else, something else, any person or any thing. Blame it on the environment, blame it on society." "It's a wonder that anyone comes out healthy, living in such a sick society." "Blame it on your parents or your mate. Whatever you do, transfer the blame away from yourself." This will relieve your sense of responsibility in the situation so that you cannot be held responsible. (Of course, you only want to apply this to the bad or wrong that you do; you want personal credit for the good!) It's true that we are all greatly affected by other people and circumstances, but a person must accept responsibility for his own actions. If he doesn't, who will?

The second method of dealing with guilt is to lower or do away with the standard or principle that was broken. "Who makes up the rules anyway?" If a person breaks the marital bond through an extra-marital affair, then let's lighten the importance of the marital bond. Take this approach to its logical end and you create a society in which everyone does whatever he decides is right. It seems this is one of the most popular themes today—"Do your own thing!" (Sometimes known as, "If it feels good, do it!") The progression in this kind of reasoning is: 1) It all depends on how you look at it, 2) It really doesn't matter how you look at it, and finally, 3) I don't think anybody knows how to look at it. Therefore, do your own thing! The result—chaos!

The third method used to deal with guilt is escape. "Move!" Where? How about central Africa? Escape—to any place you are unknown and cannot be pressured or reminded of your particular crisis situation. Without a doubt, "getting away" for a time may be helpful. But you cannot continue to run. In order to be freed from the guilt connected with a particular problem, you must face it head on. Otherwise, it will never go away, but will hide in the subconscious waiting to haunt you.

All three methods of dealing with personal guilt are not really payments of the debt at all. They are simply methods by which we ignore the problem, hoping to alleviate the "guilties." Some people find temporary relief this way, only to despair later as the cancerous beast once again raises its ugly head. Many walk away from the counseling room in despair, because they are still weighted down with the guilt and have been given no hope or relief.

There are only two ways to pay for what you have done wrong. (Your sin—the self-centered rebellion that separates you from God.) 1) You can pay for it by dying for eternity—that's a long time and hardly a possible payment. 2) You can accept God's payment of Jesus Christ's death on the cross. You see, Jesus, the God-Man, didn't come to set up another religious system, but by his death to make a payment for your sin so that you need not pay anymore. The death of the God-Man is the only payment that is adequate to pay for all of mankind's sins.

The Payoff

Let's go back to our mythical forty-foot canyon again (after recovering from our jump). Since we cannot jump it, we must find a bridge. Jesus of Nazareth, the God-Man, is the only one who can span the forty feet. He has bridged the great gap between God and man. Let's say that we just admire the bridge and discuss how truly remarkable it is. Nothing happens! There is no supernatural transference from one side to the other without actually getting on the bridge.

We must cross over that bridge. Realizing that we cannot make an adequate payment for the sin that separates us from God, and that the only adequate payment is the death of Christ (the God-Man), we must receive His payment on our behalf. That's getting on the bridge—personally counting on and receiving God's payment for your sin. It's as if a pardon were offered to a criminal on death row. He can accept it or reject it, but it will not affect his life unless he actually receives it for himself. When we receive God's payment for sin, the payoff is made.

It's at the moment of spiritual payoff that God the Holy Spirit performs His supernatural operation. He makes us dead to the power of the old nature and alive to God through our newborn spirit. In addition He resides within us Himself to provide all the power necessary to live the ultimate lifestyle.

The "criminal" evidence that a person has entered into the supernatural relationship is a gut-level feeling of peace. This is the peace that comes from having your guilt paid for. This is the peace that comes from knowing that you're not all alone in the universe. This is the peace that comes from looking through the new "glasses" God has given you which help you see that life is not out of control, but is in the hands of a personal God who cares. This is a deep inner peace.

Another element of "criminal" evidence related to peace within us is love for others. Through the supernatural revelation we are given a basis for loving people unconditionally—God's love for us. The spiritual operation gives us a new capacity to love people unconditionally.

Still another evidence of the supernatural relationship is an inner sense of destiny. This sense of destiny promises meaningfulness (abundance) in this life and heaven in the life to come. In a word, this sense of destiny gives us hope to go on living.

None of these pieces of criminal evidence can be experienced perfectly until Jesus comes again. Christianity is not synonymous with perfection. There is freedom to fail and it is a fact that we will all fail at times.

The ultimate lifestyle does not guarantee that one who lives it will always be on top of the pile. The piles will be encountered and the believer may have to go under them, around them, or even shovel through them. There may often be stress instead of peace, resentment and self-centeredness instead of unconditional love, and a sense of hopelessness instead of hope. The difference is that these times of stress, self-centeredness, and hopelessness can be relieved when the believer returns to his basis—the supernatural revelation from God. Because God is really there and cares, we can be encouraged and recharged to get back up when we fall down.

The supernatural relationship extends beyond man's vertical relationship with God to influence his horizontal relationships. As each member of the body of Christ ministers and is ministered to, God is able to meet needs, encourage the weary, heal wounds, and challenge hearts. This is the dynamic that should be taking place when the body of Christ meets together. It doesn't have to take place at a regular meeting of the church. It may just be a time of fellowship with a few friends around the dinner table. Many believers miss out on God's ministry to them because they are not looking for God in this dynamic interaction of the body. It is here that *God dynamically dwells among us.* It is here that God touches us. That's "criminal" evidence!

The supernatural relationship built upon the supernatural revelation heightens my personal confidence in the supernatural God.

Sixteen

"CRIMINAL" EVIDENCE: THE SUPERNATURAL REFLECTION!

What is it that best reveals the reality of the supernatural God to the world? What are His reflectors to man? Two of the most basic are the creation, where God's "invisible attributes, His eternal power and divine nature, have been clearly seen being understood through what has been made" (Romans 1:20), and the *conscience* of man where "that which is known about God is evident" (Romans 1:19). These two natural reflectors are solely dependent upon God. Man's response to them has nothing to do with their effectiveness.

There are at least four other reflectors of the reality of the supernatural God which are dependent upon man's response.

The Verbal Presentation of the Gospel

The first is the verbal presentation of the gospel. "Whoever will call upon the name of the Lord will be saved. How then shall they call upon Him in whom they have not believed? And how shall they believe in Him whom they have not heard? And how shall they hear without a preacher? And how shall they preach unless they are sent? Just as it is written, 'How beautiful are the feet of those who bring glad tidings of good things!' " (Romans 10:13-15).

The Lord has chosen to use the powerful living Word to penetrate the hearts of men and women, and whenever His Word goes forth, it has great effect. I heard the gospel many times before I actually received Christ as my payment for sin, but I remember the deep conviction of God that I felt on several occasions as His Word was proclaimed. The Word of God is powerfully alive and is capable of exploding in man's heart as a reflector of the supernatural God. *That's "criminal" evidence!*

The Satisfied Lifestyle

Another supernatural reflector is the satisfied lifestyle. Jesus said, "Let your light shine before men in such a way that they may see your good works, and glorify your Father who is in heaven" (Matthew 5:16). Because it's so rare, the world notices when a person has his head together. Even though a person may pretend to be an expert on how to live life, at the same time he may be listening to and watching anyone who appears to know who he is and where he is going—anyone who seems to be happy. The world's initial reaction to the happy person is generally to attack him and look for "dirt" on him, but if the believer passes the test and is truly experiencing a meaningful and satisfied lifestyle, the world will be drawn to him. This is especially true when they have observed a change in a person's life. "Is it just a phase he is going through?" When it becomes obvious that the change is for real, the supernatural reflection is crystal clear. *That's "criminal" evidence!*

Love for One Another

A third supernatural reflector is love for one another. In His last extensive meeting with His disciples before the crucifixion Jesus made a startling statement. He said, "A new commandment I give to you, that you love one another, even as I have loved you, that you also love one another. By this all men will know that you are My disciples, if you have love for one another" (John 13:34-35). Later in that same meeting He said that the disciples' oneness would cause the world to believe that He was sent by God. The active demonstration of loving one another is a rare and beautiful dynamic that reflects to the world the reality of the supernatural God. *That's "criminal" evidence!*

Returning Good for Evil

A fourth supernatural reflector is the ability to respond to an insult with a blessing. Peter makes it clear that this action will result in the non-believer asking for a "reason for the hope that is within" us. Why? Because it's so rare—so supernatural. It's the same as the reaction God had in the face of our rebellion—a blessing for an insult. *That's "criminal" evidence!*

When all four of these supernatural reflectors are operative within a body of believers at the same time, the effect can be dramatic. About three years ago I was invited to speak at a college conference in Missouri. A staff member for the conference picked me up at the airport in a large van. There were quite a few students in the van, and apparently they were not aware that I was the conference speaker. On our way to the conference center I overheard an interesting conversation in the last row of the van. A Jewish girl asked her Christian friend, "What are we going to do at this weekend conference?" Her friend answered hesitantly, "We're going to listen to a speaker." "Listen to a speaker?" she blurted out. At this point I slowly slumped down in my seat, praying for the Rapture. "About six times!" the Christian girl replied. "Six times? I can't believe it!" I could tell this was going to be an exciting conference.

That night at the first session the Jewish girl sat in the back and left within the first few minutes of my message. At each of the next two sessions she stayed progressively longer.

On Saturday night she stayed the entire time. Later that evening, she walked up to me like a Sherman tank and said, "I want to know something right now. Why is it that everybody here seems to love each other so much? Everybody's so darn nice! Back at the university a person could practically knock you down and you'd never hear a word, but here, even when someone just brushes against you, you hear 'Excuse me! Excuse me!' I just don't get it. Why are these people so different?" When I finally got a chance to speak, I said, "I don't think you'd want to know the answer, so I'm not going to say." She came right back at me, "Do you mean Jesus?" I shook my head in the affirmative direction without saying anything. She said, "Don't give me this Jesus business! I want to know what makes the difference between these students and those back at the university!" Here was a girl who was overwhelmed with the supernatural reflection and demanded to know the reason behind the reflectors. As we continued to talk, she opened up to the point of wanting to hear how she could accept Jesus as her Messiah. *That's "criminal" evidence!*

It's almost as though each member of the body of Christ is a piece of a puzzle. Each piece has protrusions and indentations. The protrusions might be the strengths and the indentations, the weaknesses. Some people's strengths fit and fill up others' weaknesses. As the pieces begin to come together, a beautiful picture becomes visible to those around. It is a picture of Jesus—the supernatural revelation of God offering a supernatural relationship to the world.

As we continue craving the supernatural God and His ultimate lifestyle, our relationship with Him must display true reality and offer genuine hope to the world. *Reality* is experienced through a dynamic interaction with the supernatural revelation (both the written Word and the living Word). *Hope* is expressed to the world through the supernatural reflections of the supernatural God.

If Christianity were a crime, would there be enough evidence to convict *you*?

Appendix One

PRIORITIES ARE FOR PEOPLE

Charles R. Buxton was the one who first said, "You will never 'find' time for anything. If you want time you must make it." Another has said, "We are always complaining that our days are few, and acting as though there would be no end to them." We are all given a fixed amount of time. It is for us to decide how to spend it.

Priorities refer to quality of time rather than quantity. A priority item is an important one that must precede lesser ones in our time and attention. Most people are too busy, always under extreme pressure to get things done. With few exceptions each one of us is wrestling with what to do next rather than with what is to be done ultimately.

We need a priority grid in order to make decisions that will produce *peace* and not *pressure*. Some of the most intense pressures in life are created by our inability to say No with confidence that we are right. The result? Either a person is intimidated into saying Yes to something that warrants a No, or he is burdened down with guilt after blurting out an unsettled No. Either approach creates pressure. There may be pressure created by doing too much, or pressure arising from the guilt of saying No.

A proper priority grid will free you from unnecessary pressures. I used to feel guilty for taking a day off or for turning a ministry request down. But not any more. I have a new freedom to say No based on my priority grid.

Although the Bible doesn't set forth a priority grid for us in five or six steps, such a grid can be constructed from the Bible with an understanding of various passages. The most basic of these passages is John 15. Here Jesus instructs His disciples concerning the relationships of life in three general categories. In verses 1-11 He discusses the believer's relationship with Christ Himself. He uses the figure of the vine—Jesus—and the branches—believers. This relationship is to be characterized by abiding in Him. Verses 12-17 present the believer's relationship with other believers. This relationship is to be characterized by loving one another. In the last section (18-27) Jesus describes the world's hate and disgust at believers because of their identification with Him. In verses 26 and 27 He says: "When the Helper comes . . . He will bear witness of Me, and you will bear witness also, because you have been with Me from the beginning." This is to be the believer's relationship with the world, characterized by bearing witness of Jesus.

These three categories of relationships are used throughout the New Testament. They are presented as high priorities for the Christian life. John 15 teaches that the most important action for the believer is to abide in Christ. Then he is to love other believers actively and to bear witness to the world. The closer his relationship with Christ the better will be his relationships with other believers. The closer his relationship with Christ and other believers the more effective will be his relationship with the world as a witness for Christ.

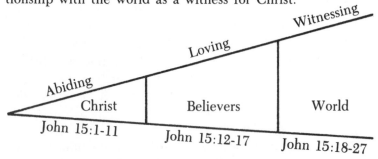

Abiding — Christ — John 15:1-11
Loving — Believers — John 15:12-17
Witnessing — World — John 15:18-27

A proper priority grid cannot be developed without an understanding of these basic relationships emphasized in the Bible.

Other passages that add insight into priorities are found in the pastoral epistles of I and II Timothy and Titus. Paul lists qualifications for spiritual leadership and ministry. These qualifications are primarily qualities of lifestyle rather than abilities. They can easily be placed into the three categories of relationships that Jesus discussed in John 15, qualities in relationship to Jesus, in relationship to fellow believers (including family), and in relationship to the world. All of these qualify a person for ministry to others. Although the passage is specifically speaking of elders, deacons, and deaconesses, it serves as an excellent guideline for setting up a biblical priority grid.

Priority 1: The cultivation of a personal relationship with the Lord.

This is your walk with God—not your ministry for Him. For quite some time I've been disturbed at how Christians like to appear religious. We tell the non-believer that Christianity is not a religious system of do's and don'ts, but that it is a relationship with God. Then as soon as that person becomes a believer we force him into being very religious. "You must come to these services. Then there is a prayer group which meets on Thursday that you should attend. Oh, yes, you need to have a quiet time—just five or six minutes a day will be fine. Just be sure to check in with the Lord." These, and many more rules bury the new believer in "religiosity" and rob him of the natural development of a relationship with God.

Suppose I were to tell you that I have an outstanding relationship with my wife, and this is the way it works: at 6:30 in the morning we wake up, I say to my wife, "Honey, tonight from 6:00 to 6:30 is your time with me—be there!" That is not a relationship. At best it's an acquaintanceship! It seems that throughout Christianity too many are experiencing a "relationship" with God that is only an acquaintanceship—a nod to God at religious moments or at crisis points.

A relationship with God must be cultivated like any other relationship. There must be communication: talking (prayer to God) and listening (through God's written revelation). The more you communicate the more you know about Him and what pleases Him. So you seek to please Him by doing His will.

Priority 2: The cultivation of a personal relationship with your mate.

After your relationship with God, the second most important relationship is with your mate. Many men find it easy to allow their vocation or ministry to slip into this second slot. On the other hand, women frequently place their children or home in second place.

For a long time in our marriage I didn't take a real day off because "I was in the ministry." As my conference schedule and counseling load continued to increase, the pressures on my wife and on our relationship became overwhelming. Even though I thought the Lord's work could not be accomplished without my seven-day-a-week input, I decided to experiment with a real day off. No office mail or calls! No counseling over the phone! No preparation of messages! No writing of books or articles! It was amazing to see what happened. The Lord's work has continued, and my ministry is more effective. My wife is more excited about life, and our relationship has become more creative and refreshing.

I've talked with many men over the years who complain of their wives being extremely negative and naggingly resistant when the husband wants to go out with the guys—hunting or golfing or playing tennis. In such cases the wife is not necessarily down on hunting or golfing or tennis but is screaming for his attention to the priorities of the marriage. In each situation I've counseled the man to evaluate and rework his priorities—emphasizing his need to cultivate an intimate, personal relationship with his wife. After this foundation is laid in the relationship, the wife may lose her need to be resistant and negative. In some cases she may even become excited about your activity.

Priority 3: The cultivation of a personal relationship with your children.

Without a doubt the three most important aspects of parenthood are relationship, relationship, and then relationship. I'm convinced that parents could fail miserably in the area of discipline, being either too permissive or too authoritarian, and still succeed if there is a healthy relationship.

Although priorities have to do with quality of time more than quantity of time, we should be careful not to use that as a cop-out in our relationship with our children. Relationships take time, so plan to spend time relating to each child individually every week.

Priority 4: The cultivation of personal relationships inside the body of Christ.

Just as God decided that it is "not good" for a person to be alone, leading to His establishment of the marital relationship, so He established the church to deal with the problem of aloneness in living the Christian life. Paul makes it clear in his letter to the Ephesian church that normal spiritual growth only takes place as each individual part of the body is fitted together and functions properly.

The Lord touches or ministers to people's needs primarily through His Word and through His people. Just as we are to receive our mates as a gift from God to complete us, so we are to receive other members of the body of believers as gifts of God for our fulfillment. Notice that there is a difference between "accepting" a person as he/she is and "receiving" a person as an ambassador of God (a believer-priest) to us.

Jesus viewed this priority highly. He said that if this priority were in operation, the world would know that He was in reality sent by God.

Priority 5: The cultivation of personal relationships outside the body of Christ.

Paul says that we should have a "good reputation" with those outside the body of believers. Your vocation as well as your general conduct in business dealings should be included here. Your relationship with neighbors, relatives, organizations, etc. are extremely important. We are told to separate ourselves, but not isolate ourselves, from the world. We are separate in that believers have a standard of righteousness and a relationship with God (light) as opposed to the unbeliever's unrighteousness and no relationship with God (darkness). We are to be open Bibles for them to read and examine so that they may find the God of the universe. They cannot read us unless we come a little closer!

Priority 6: The cultivation of personal ministry relationships.

The first five priorities qualify you for ministry in the more formal sense of the word. This may, of course, take different forms—teaching, preaching, leading, administration, etc.

Unfortunately, this priority often shoulders its way upward to a higher position on the priority list than it should have. Somehow it seems so easy to justify ministry activity at any cost. But there is no justification possible when the cost may be your relationship with God or your family. You should disqualify yourself from ministry if your first five priorities aren't in order.

Priorities free you to live life according to God's game plan.

Appendix Two

THE "HAIRY" WORLD OF THE NON-ABSOLUTES!

Absolutes, non-absolutes, and personal convictions! Fuzziness in the distinctions among these three terms continues to cause frustration, guilt, confusion, and division within the body of Christ. *Absolutes* are for everyone, everywhere, all the time and are specifically delineated within Scripture. There is no variableness in an absolute. An example would be that we should love one another. *Non-absolutes* are not for everyone, everywhere, all the time and are not specified within Scripture. Non-absolutes are relative—they are neither right nor wrong in and of themselves. Examples of non-absolutes would be dancing or attending movies. *Personal convictions* are really personal "absolutes." It's an absolute that is not for everyone, but for the person himself. Personal convictions are not directly revealed from God to man, but are derived within the context of the person's own response to God's revelation.

There are two dangerously wrong tendencies—the tendency to make absolutes out of non-absolutes and the tendency to make absolutes out of personal convictions.

First, the tendency to make absolutes out of non-absolutes. There are many non-absolutes within the Christian world that are treated as if they were in the book of absolutes. The absolutizing of non-absolutes varies according to cultural contexts. For instance, in some areas of the country attending movies is considered to be absolutely wrong. But in other areas of the same fellowship or denomination of Christians, nothing is seen to be wrong with attending movies, with obvious discrimination necessary. There are some communities of believers that teach that skating is absolutely wrong, whereas most believers would not even think of skating as being a sin.

There is a strong compulsion within us to try to label everything as black or white. But life is not just black and white. God has revealed to us absolute precepts and principles that must be followed, but there are areas in which God has not given absolutes.

The tendency of making absolutes out of non-absolutes spills over into the application of biblical principles as well. Biblical precepts and principles are absolute and must be applied by every believer, but to teach or to imply by your teaching that there is an absolute way to apply the absolutes of God is very wrong. Every person and situation is different and the absolute Word of God must be applied in different ways.

In observing various seminars throughout the country I have found that little distinction is made between the absolute principles of God and the non-absolute opinions of the teacher as to how God's absolutes are to be applied. Since there is a strong tendency to have everything down in black and white categories, people leave these seminars with a false security in the "ten steps to do this" or the "seven steps to do that." These steps may be good (maybe the best), but they are not the only way for everyone to apply a given principle of God. The steps are nothing more than wise suggestions. They are non-absolutes and must not be viewed as absolute.

The real danger in making absolutes out of non-absolutes is that a false picture of Christianity is presented to the world and a false model of the Christian lifestyle to believers. The world sees just another religious system of do's and don'ts and cannot see the real "criminal" evidence of true Christianity. The believers follow the model of the religious system and do not experience the "criminal" evidence in their rela-

tionship with the supernatural God. The result? A poor caricature of Christianity is experienced by the believer and
observed by the world. In most cases the believer and the non-
believer miss the reality of Christianity. The non-believer rejects it by simply turning it off as you might turn off your tele-
vision set when something distasteful comes on. The believer
passively accepts this kind of religious non-Christianity by
becoming embalmed in the whole religious system, never
expecting to discover any more reality.

*Second, the tendency to make absolutes out of personal
convictions.* Personal convictions are *personal absolutes* not
universal absolutes. In the area of non-absolutes (where God
has not revealed specific instructions) each believer must
make personal decisions whether to act or not to act—to dance
or not to dance, to attend movies or not to attend movies, to
skate or not to skate, to drink or not to drink, to eat meat sacri-
ficed to idols or not, etc.

If I come to the conviction that I should not dance (for
whatever reason), I must not enforce this personal conviction
on everyone else (as an absolute). That personal conviction is
between God and me. If I come to the conviction that I should
not buy anything on Sunday, I must not restrict everyone's activity on that day. If I come to the conviction that I should
meditate on the Word in a certain way and at a certain time of
day, I must not place everyone else in the same mold or on the
same performance level. *Personal convictions are personal!*

Freedom in Christ

The Bible teaches complete freedom in Christ in the
areas of the non-absolutes. "One man has faith that he may
eat all things, but he who is weak eats vegetables only. *Let not
him who eats regard with contempt him who does not eat, and
let not him who does not eat judge him who eats*, for God has
accepted him. Who are you to judge the servant of another?
To his own master he stands or falls; and stand he will, for the
Lord is able to make him stand. One man regards one day

above another, another regards every day alike. Let each man be fully convinced in his own mind. He who observes the day, observes it for the Lord, and he who eats, does so for the Lord, for he gives thanks to God, and he who eats not, for the Lord he does not eat, and gives thanks to God.

"For not one of us lives for himself, and not one dies for himself; for if we live, we live for the Lord, or if we die, we die for the Lord; therefore whether we live or die, we are the Lord's.

"For to this end Christ died and lived again, that He might be Lord both of the dead and of the living. But you, why do you judge your brother? Or you again, why do you regard your brother with contempt? For we shall all stand before the judgment-seat of God. For it is written, 'As I live, says the Lord, every knee shall bow to me, and every tongue shall give praise to God.' So then each one of us shall give account of himself to God" (Romans 14:2-12).

No Offense to a Brother

"Therefore, let us not judge one another any more, but rather determine this—not to put an obstacle or a stumblingblock in a brother's way. I am convinced in the Lord Jesus that nothing is unclean in itself; but to him who thinks anything to be unclean, to him it is unclean. For if because of food your brother is hurt, you are no longer walking according to love. Do not destroy with your food him for whom Christ died.

"Therefore do not let what is for you a good thing be spoken of as evil; for the kingdom of God is not eating and drinking, but righteousness and peace and joy in the Holy Spirit. For he who in this way serves Christ is acceptable to God and approved by men. So then let us pursue the things which make for peace and the building up of one another. Do not tear down the work of God for the sake of food. All things indeed are clean, but they are evil for the man who eats and gives offence. It is good not to eat meat or drink wine, or to do anything by which your brother stumbles.

"The faith which you have, have as your own conviction before God. Happy is he who does not condemn himself in what he approves. But he who doubts is condemned if he eats, because his eating is not from faith; and whatever is not from faith is sin.

"Now we who are strong ought to bear the weaknesses of those without strength and not just please ourselves. Let each of us please his neighbor for his good, to his edification" (Romans 14:13-15:2).

Glory to God

"Whether, then, you eat or drink or whatever you do, do all to the glory of God" (I Corinthians 10:31). "Now may the God who gives perseverance and encouragement grant you to be of the same mind with one another according to Christ Jesus; that with one accord you may with one voice glorify the God and Father of our Lord Jesus Christ. Wherefore, accept one another, just as Christ also accepted us to the glory of God" (Romans 15:5-7).

These three principles—freedom in Christ, giving no offense, and glory to God—will help sort out the hairy world of non-absolutes and enable you to experience and express true Christianity.